AMERICAN POLITICAL, ECONOMIC, AND SECURITY ISSUES

HILLARY RODHAM CLINTON (HRC) PAID SPEECHES

AMERICAN POLITICAL, ECONOMIC, AND SECURITY ISSUES

Additional books in this series can be found on Nova's website
under the Series tab.

Additional e-books in this series can be found on Nova's website
under the e-books tab.

AMERICAN POLITICAL, ECONOMIC, AND SECURITY ISSUES

HILLARY RODHAM CLINTON (HRC) PAID SPEECHES

CHRISTIAN MELLOR

Copyright © 2018 by Nova Science Publishers, Inc.

All rights reserved. No part of this book may be reproduced, stored in a retrieval system or transmitted in any form or by any means: electronic, electrostatic, magnetic, tape, mechanical photocopying, recording or otherwise without the written permission of the Publisher.

We have partnered with Copyright Clearance Center to make it easy for you to obtain permissions to reuse content from this publication. Simply navigate to this publication's page on Nova's website and locate the "Get Permission" button below the title description. This button is linked directly to the title's permission page on copyright.com. Alternatively, you can visit copyright.com and search by title, ISBN, or ISSN.

For further questions about using the service on copyright.com, please contact:
Copyright Clearance Center
Phone: +1-(978) 750-8400   Fax: +1-(978) 750-4470   E-mail: info@copyright.com.

NOTICE TO THE READER

The Publisher has taken reasonable care in the preparation of this book, but makes no expressed or implied warranty of any kind and assumes no responsibility for any errors or omissions. No liability is assumed for incidental or consequential damages in connection with or arising out of information contained in this book. The Publisher shall not be liable for any special, consequential, or exemplary damages resulting, in whole or in part, from the readers' use of, or reliance upon, this material. Any parts of this book based on government reports are so indicated and copyright is claimed for those parts to the extent applicable to compilations of such works.

Independent verification should be sought for any data, advice or recommendations contained in this book. In addition, no responsibility is assumed by the publisher for any injury and/or damage to persons or property arising from any methods, products, instructions, ideas or otherwise contained in this publication.

This publication is designed to provide accurate and authoritative information with regard to the subject matter covered herein. It is sold with the clear understanding that the Publisher is not engaged in rendering legal or any other professional services. If legal or any other expert assistance is required, the services of a competent person should be sought. FROM A DECLARATION OF PARTICIPANTS JOINTLY ADOPTED BY A COMMITTEE OF THE AMERICAN BAR ASSOCIATION AND A COMMITTEE OF PUBLISHERS.

Additional color graphics may be available in the e-book version of this book.

Library of Congress Cataloging-in-Publication Data

ISBN: 978-1-53613-794-1

Published by Nova Science Publishers, Inc. † New York

CONTENTS

Preface		ix
Chapter 1	Awkward	1
Chapter 2	Benghazi/Libya	3
Chapter 3	Big Government	7
Chapter 4	Budget	9
Chapter 5	Campaign Contributions	11
Chapter 6	China	15
Chapter 7	Clinton Foundation	23
Chapter 8	Cruz, Ted	27
Chapter 9	Cuba	29
Chapter 10	Cybersecurity	31
Chapter 11	Debt Limit	35
Chapter 12	Education	37
Chapter 13	Egypt	39

Chapter 14	Equal Pay	47
Chapter 15	Email	49
Chapter 16	Emanuel, Rahm	53
Chapter 17	Energy	57
Chapter 18	Europe	71
Chapter 19	Government Surveillance	73
Chapter 20	Guns	81
Chapter 21	Haiti	83
Chapter 22	Health Care	85
Chapter 23	Helping Corporations	97
Chapter 24	Housing	105
Chapter 25	Immigration	109
Chapter 26	Income Inequality	113
Chapter 27	Iran	119
Chapter 28	Islam	125
Chapter 29	Israel	127
Chapter 30	Japan	129
Chapter 31	Marijuana	131
Chapter 32	Mexico	133
Chapter 33	Media	135
Chapter 34	North Korea	137
Chapter 35	Personal Stories	139
Chapter 36	Personal Wealth	141
Chapter 37	Pivot to Asia	143

Chapter 38	Politics	**145**
Chapter 39	Pro-Free Trade	**155**
Chapter 40	Reducing Regulations	**165**
Chapter 41	Refugees	**167**
Chapter 42	Russia	**169**
Chapter 43	Shanghai Expo	**173**
Chapter 44	Simpson-Bowles	**175**
Chapter 45	Syria	**179**
Chapter 46	Taxes	**191**
Chapter 47	Technology/New Economy	**195**
Chapter 48	Terrorism	**197**
Chapter 49	Unpaid Internships	**199**
Chapter 50	Wall Street	**201**
Chapter 51	Wal-Mart	**213**
Index		**221**

PREFACE*

This book is a compilation of speeches of the former Secretary of State, Hillary Clinton. This includes topics on:

- Benghazi/Libya
- China
- Campaign Contributions
- Egypt
- Government Surveillance
- Haiti
- Russia
- Taxes
- Personal Wealth
- North Korea
- Mexico
- Syria
- Islam

And much more. The information included in this book was initially released by WikiLeaks, the international non-profit organization that was launched in 2006 for the purposes of disseminating original documents from anonymous sources.

---

* This is an edited, reformatted and augmented version of "HRC Paid Speeches" originally published by WikiLeaks.

Chapter 1

AWKWARD

When a Questioner at Goldman Sachs Said She Raised Money for Hillary Clinton in 2008, Hillary Clinton Joked "You Are the Smartest People."

"PARTICIPANT: Secretary, Ann Chow from Houston, Texas. I have had the honor to raise money for you when you were running for president in Texas. MS. CLINTON: You are the smartest people. PARTICIPANT: I think you actually called me on my cell phone, too. I talked to you afterwards." [Speech to Goldman Sachs, 2013 IBD CEO Annual Conference, 6/4/13]

Hillary Clinton Joked That If Lloyd Blankfein Wanted to Run for Office, He Should "Would Leave Goldman Sachs and Start Running a Soup Kitchen Somewhere."

"MR. BLANKFEIN: I'm saying for myself. MS. CLINTON: If you were going to run here is what I would tell you to do—MR. BLANKFEIN: Very hypothetical.

MS. CLINTON: I think you would leave Goldman Sachs and start running a soup kitchen somewhere.

MR. BLANKFEIN: For one thing the stock would go up. MS. CLINTON: Then you could be a legend in your own time both when you were there and when you left." [Speech to Goldman Sachs, 2013 IBD CEO Annual Conference, 6/4/13]

Hillary Clinton Noted President Clinton Had Spoken at the Same Goldman Summit Last Year, and Blankfein Joked "He Increased Our Budget."

"SECRETARY CLINTON: Well, first, thanks for having me here and giving me a chance to know a little bit more about the builders and the innovators who you've gathered. Some of you might have been here last year, and my husband was, I guess, in this very same position. And he came back and was just thrilled by—MR. BLANKFEIN: He increased our budget. SECRETARY CLINTON: Did he? MR. BLANKFEIN: Yes. That's why we—SECRETARY CLINTON: Good. I think he—I think he encouraged you to grow it a little, too. But it really was a tremendous experience for him, so I've been looking forward to it and hope we have a chance to talk about a lot of things." [Goldman Sachs Builders and Innovators Summit, 10/29/13]

Chapter 2

BENGHAZI/LIBYA

Hillary Clinton Discussed Libya's Struggles after Gaddafi's Fall.

"In Libya, they had one of the best elections in the whole region after the fall of Gaddafi, but they've not been able to assert control over the security of their nation in any way yet. So they have a lot of the right impulses and desires, but don't know how to move the levers of authority to provide security for citizens, business interests and the like." [Hamilton College Speech, 10/4/13]

Clinton Said Libya Was a Challenging Situation and That Benghazi Was Very Much on Her Mind.

"Libya is a very challenging situation for everybody. There the people of Libya wanted help. Neither the United States nor Arab countries imposed their campaign against Gaddafi on them. They were demonstrating. He was going after them. We helped in an unprecedented coalition between NATO and the Arab League. Gaddafi is thrown off, but, remember, this is a man who did not permit any institution to be firmly established. He didn't have an army because he came out of the army, and he knew that if he had an army somebody like him might come out after him. So he had mercenaries, and militias were heavily armed, largely with the weaponry they stole from Gaddafi's storehouses. They had an election, which was really a promising election, broad cross-section of people elected, but they're insecure, and a government's first job is to secure its people, and they can't figure out how to do it, and it's a big debate in our country and Europe what can we do to help them because, you know, obviously I'm sitting up here with Benghazi very much, you know, in my mind. You try to help, you try to create relationships, and, you know, the hard guys with the guns have a different idea. So if you don't have overwhelming force, it's difficult. So Libya is an open book yet." [Clinton Speech For General Electric's Global Leadership Meeting—Boca Raton, FL, 1/6/14]

Clinton Discussed Lack of Institutions in Libya after Gaddafi's Fall.

"Now, you know, in Libya, the United Nations voted how to protect civilians. And the coalition that was put together was unprecedented. It was NATO plus the Arab League. That had never happened before. The over flights, the boat, air, sea, and land efforts included Arab nations as well as Europeans, Canadians and Americans. Khadafy was told but then, you know, the lid was taken off. You have a country that had been under the thumb of Khadafy and his henchmen for 42 years. All institutions were destroyed. There was not even a military because he didn't trust anybody since he had been a Colonel who had done a coup, so he had mercenaries, there were African mercenaries and some European mercenaries that were in his direct pay. They had really just conducted themselves as if the entire Libyan oil fortune was personally theirs." [Clinton Remarks at Boston Consulting Group, 6/20/13]

Benghazi/Libya

Clinton Said Libya Could Not Provide Security "As We Found Much To, You Know, Our Terrible Experience in Benghazi."

"So what happened? Well, Khadafy is gone. They start to organize. They had one of the best elections that any of these new countries had. They did not elect extremists. They had a very good outcome of people representing the various factions, but they didn't, they don't have a military. They can't provide security as we found much to, you know, our terrible experience in Benghazi, but we see it all over the country. So the jury is out but it is not for lack of trying by the people who have inherited the positions of responsibility." [Clinton Remarks at Boston Consulting Group, 6/20/13]

Clinton: "My Biggest Regret Is the Loss of Our Four Americans in Benghazi with the Attack on Our Mission, Our Post There."

"My biggest regret is the loss of our four Americans in Benghazi with the attack on our mission, our post there. It wasn't a consulate. That was ~I knew the ambassador. I had sent him there. I had picked him as someone during the Libyan revolution to actually go to Benghazi, because he understood Libya, he spoke great Arabic and French. And he built relationships with a lot of the local people. And of course it was just devastating that there was this attack on our post and on our CIA annex, which I can talk about now, because it's all been made public. And that the kind of reliability that governments have to count on from the governments in which they operate, like we're responsible for the security ultimately of every embassy in Washington. Well, the Libyan government has no capacity to deliver and the people that we had contracted with were incapable or unwilling to do it. So that was a deep regret. And you learn from these events, just as we have over the last 30-plus years, where embassies have been attacked or taken over, or the terrible events in Beirut in 1983-84. You learn from them, but it always comes down to this very hard choice, should

6   *Christian Mellor*

American civilians be in dangerous places?" [Remarks at Cisco, 8/28/14]

Hillary Clinton Said the Worst Event on Her Watch Was Benghazi, Saying It Was Motivated by "Militias as the Others in Eastern Libya."

"Well, the worst thing that happened on my watch was Benghazi. There is no doubt about that. It was a terrible, tragic event that, you know, was motivated by, you know, the militias and the others in eastern Libya and in which, unfortunately, you know, killed four brave Americans, including one Chris Stevens, who I knew quite well. I had sent him as a diplomat to Benghazi during the Libyan uprising. He had served there. He spoke flawless Arabic. He knew a lot of the people. He had been in Tripoli as our what's called Deputy Chief Of Mission, DCM. We had to close the embassy because Gaddafi and his thugs were threatening our diplomats. So Chris was back home, and when we saw what was happening, I said, 'You know, we need somebody to connect with the uprising, the rebels, the militias.' He held up his hand. He volunteered. He went to Benghazi during the war, came back. I recommended him for ambassador. Of course the President agreed. So he was out in Tripoli. He really knew the country as well as any American and assessed that it was important for him not to just be behind the walls, but to get out, and, you know, really connect with Libyan leaders and citizens. And it was just a terrible crime that he was killed doing what was really in the best interests of both the United States and Libya." [Hillary Clinton remarks to Global Business Travelers Association, 8/7/13]

Chapter 3

BIG GOVERNMENT

Clinton: "My Father Raised Me to Be Suspicious of Big Everything, Big Government, Big Business, Big Anything."

"I'll just end by, you know, my father was a rock-ribbed republican, he and my mother always split the votes, they started what is called the gender gap in American politics, but my father raised me to be suspicious of big everything, big government, big business, big anything, you know, people lose touch with what really is happening if they're not held accountable, if they don't have the right information because it can't get to them, you are going to run into problems. And so for me growing up with a small businessman father in the middle west, having great experiences I've had in practicing law, in teaching law, in working on public company boards and certainly, you know, serving in many not for profit as well as public service positions, running for office, holding office, winning, losing, yeah, I come out of it all even more optimistic about our country, but I'm well aware that we have to get our act together, and by getting our act together, we will be able to look at the next hundred years as an American century that will have benefits for all of us, and that's really my core conviction and what I will spend my time trying to contribute to for the years to come." [Hillary Clinton remarks at Sanford Bernstein, 5/29/13]

Chapter 4

BUDGET

Hillary Clinton: "You've Got to Have Spending Restraints and You've Got to Have Some Revenues in Order to Stimulate Growth."

"And there are other ways that we can put ourselves on a better footing, like passing a decent immigration law and dealing with our budget and being smart about it and realizing there is two sides to the equation. You've got to have spending restraints and you've got to have some revenues in order to stimulate growth." [Speech to Goldman Sachs, 2013 IBD CEO Annual Conference, 6/4/13]

Chapter 5

Campaign Contributions

Clinton Said That Because Candidates Needed Money from Wall Street to Run for Office, People in New York Needed to Ask Tough Questions about the Economy before Handing over Campaign Contributions.

"Secondly, running for office in our country takes a lot of money, and candidates have to go out and raise it. New York is probably the leading site for contributions for fundraising for candidates on both sides of the aisle, and it's also our economic center. And there are a lot of people here who should ask some tough questions before handing over campaign contributions to people who were really playing chicken with our whole economy." [Goldman Sachs AIMS Alternative Investments Symposium, 10/24/13]

Clinton: "It Would Be Very Difficult to Run for President without Raising a Huge Amount of Money and without Having Other People Supporting You Because Your Opponent Will Have Their Supporters."

"So our system is, in many ways, more difficult, certainly far more expensive and much longer than a parliamentary system, and I really admire the people who subject themselves to it. Even when I, you know, think they should not be elected president, I still think, well, you know, good for you I guess, you're out there promoting democracy and those crazy ideas of yours. So I think that it's something—I would like —you know, obviously as somebody who has been through it, I would like it not to last as long because I think it's very distracting from what we should be doing every day in our public business. I would like it not to be so expensive. I have no idea how you do that. I mean, in my campaign—I lose track, but I think I raised $250 million or some such enormous amount, and in the last campaign President Obama raised 1.1 billion, and that was before the Super PACs and all of this other money just rushing in, and it's so ridiculous that we have this kind of free for all with all of this financial interest at stake, but, you know, the Supreme Court said that's basically what we're in for. So we're kind of in the Wild West, and, you know, it would be very difficult to run for president without raising a huge amount of money and without having other people supporting you because your opponent will have their supporters. So I think as hard as it was when I ran, I think it's even harder now." [Clinton Speech for General Electric's Global Leadership Meeting—Boca Raton, FL, 1/6/14]

2013: Hillary Clinton Said Someone Running for President in 2016 Would Need to Be Raising Money "Sometime Next Year or Early the Following the Year."

"So let's give some space and some attention to these issues instead of who is going to run and what they're going to do and: Oh, my gosh. What is happening tomorrow? But if someone were going to run, given the process of raising money, given the—you know, for better or worse I apparently have about a hundred percent name recognition. Most of it my mother would say is not true, but I live with it. So for me it might be slightly different than for somebody else, but you certainly would have

Campaign Contributions

to be in raising money sometime next year or early the following year." [Speech to Goldman Sachs, 2013 IBD CEO Annual Conference, 6/4/13]

Hillary Clinton Said She Admired Peter King Because He Told New York Donors to Not Give Money to Republicans Who Voted against Sandy Aid.

"MS. CLINTON: Well, you know, I really admire Peter King. He's a Republican representative from Long Island. He and I did a lot of work together after 9/11 on terrorism and all of that. But when the vote on Sandy came up—and a lot of Republicans voted against aid for New York and New Jersey, Peter King said to the New York funders: Don't give any of them any money because somehow you have to get their attention. So I thought it was pretty clever. I know what it's like. I mean, everybody is New York on Mondays." [Speech to Goldman Sachs, 2013 IBD CEO Annual Conference, 6/4/13]

Hillary Clinton Said Politicians Treat NYC like an ATM and "Political Givers" Need to Tell Politicians "Here Are Things I Want You to Do for the Country.

"So I think that we're going to have to take seriously how we fund disasters, but I think Peter's point was a larger one, which is—you know, New York is kind of an ATM machine for both Democrats and Republicans, and people come up and they visit with many of you and they ask for money, and often they're given—if they're coming they're going to get it. And at some point the American public—and particularly political givers—have to say: Here—and it's not just about me. It's not just about my personal standings. Here are things I want you to do for the country and be part of that debate about the country." [Speech to Goldman Sachs, 2013 IBD CEO Annual Conference, 6/4/13]

14 *Christian Mellor*

Hillary Clinton: "Those Who Help to Fund Elections, I Think It's Important That Business Leaders Make It Clear, Why Would You Give Money to Somebody Who Was Willing to Wreck the Full Faith and Credit of the United States."

"And then it comes down to who we vote for and what kind of expectations we set and who we give money to. Those who help to fund elections, I think it's important that business leaders make it clear, why would you give money to somebody who was willing to wreck the full faith and credit of the United States. I mean, that just makes no sense at all because the economic repercussions would have been very bad, and the long-term consequences with, you know, the Chinese saying, let's de-Americanize the world and eventually move to a different reserve currency wouldn't be, you know, beneficial, either." [Goldman Sachs Builders and Innovators Summit, 10/29/13]

Chapter 6

CHINA

Clinton Praised the New President of China Xi Jinping as "Much More Sophisticated" Than Hu Jintao, Praised His "Far-Reaching" Plans for Economic and Social Reform.

"Well, I think it is such a consequential relationship. And the new president of China is a much more sophisticated actor than his predecessor. He lived in the United States for a short period of time, actually lived in Iowa on a—on a farm. He was working in agricultural issues within the Communist party, you know, about 30 years ago. He is a better politician than his immediate predecessor, Hu Jintao. He has consolidated his power quite quickly over the military and over the Communist party. He has set forth a plan for economic reform, some of which is quite far-reaching, and some social reform as well like, you know, saying they're going to end, at least to some extent, the one-child policy." [Remarks to CME Group, 11/18/13]

Hillary Clinton Called Xi Jingping "He's a More Sophisticated, More Effective Public Leader Than Hu Jintao Was."

"I think it's a good news/maybe not so good news story about what is going on right now in China. On the good news side I think the new leadership—and we'll see more of that when Xi Jinping gets here in the United States after having gone to Latin America. He's a more sophisticated, more effective public leader than Hu Jintao was. He is political in the kind of generic sense of that word. You can see him work a room, which I have watched him do. You can have him make small talk with you, which he has done with me. His experience as a young man coming to the United States in the 1980s—going to Iowa, spending time there, living with a family—was a very important part of his own development." [Speech to Goldman Sachs, 2013 IBD CEO Annual Conference, 6/4/13]

Hillary Clinton Said "He Understands the Different Levers and the Constituencies That He Has to Work with Internally and Externally."

"So he's someone who you at least have the impression is a more worldly, somewhat more experienced politician. And I say that as a term of praise, because he understands the different levers and the constituencies that he has to work with internally and externally. That's especially important because of the recent moves he's making to consolidate power over the military." [Speech to Goldman Sachs, 2013 IBD CEO Annual Conference, 6/4/13]

Hillary Clinton Said Chinese Leaders Don't like People Knowing Most of Their Children Attend American Universities.

"MR. BLANKFEIN: His daughter is at Harvard? MS. CLINTON: Yes. They don't like you to know that, but most of the Chinese leadership children are at American universities or have been. I said to one very, very high ranking Chinese official about a year, year and a half ago—I said: I understand your daughter went to Wellesley. He said: Who told you? I said: Okay. I don't have to punish the person then." [Speech to Goldman Sachs, 2013 IBD CEO Annual Conference, 6/4/13]

China 17

Hillary Clinton Said "President Xi Is Doing Much More to Try to Assert His Authority, and I Think That Is Also Good News."

"One of the biggest concerns I had over the last four years was the concern that was manifested several different ways that the PLA, the People's Liberation Army, was acting somewhat independently; that it wasn't just a good cop/bad cop routine when we would see some of the moves and some of the rhetoric coming out of the PLA, but that in effect that were making some foreign policy. And Hu Jintao, unlike Jiang Zemin before him, never really captured the authority over the PLA that is essential for any government, whether it's a civilian government in our country or a communist party government in China. So President Xi is doing much more to try to assert his authority, and I think that is also good news." [Speech to Goldman Sachs, 2013 IBD CEO Annual Conference, 6/4/13]

Hillary Clinton Warned of Rising Nationalism in China, Saying "I Had High Chinese Officials in Their 60s and 50s Say to Me: We All Know Somebody Who Was Killed by the Japanese during the War."

"On the not so good side there is a resurgence of nationalism inside China that is being at least condoned, if not actively pushed by the new Chinese government. You know, Xi Jinping talks about the Chinese dream, which he means to be kind of the Chinese version of the American dream. There has been a stoking of residual anti-Japanese feelings inside China, not only in the leadership but in the populace. It's ostensibly over the dispute that is ongoing, but it's deeper than that and it is something that bears very careful watching. Because in my last year, year and a half of meetings with the highest officials in China the rhetoric about the Japanese was vicious, and I had high Chinese officials in their 60s and 50s say to me: We all know somebody who was killed by the Japanese during the war. We cannot let them resume their nationalistic ways. You Americans are naive. You don't see what is happening below the surface of Japan society." [Speech to Goldman Sachs, 2013 IBD CEO Annual Conference, 6/4/13]

Hillary Clinton Said "the Biggest Supporters of a Provocative North Korea Has Been the PLA."

"Now, that looks back to an important connection of what I said before. The biggest supporters of a provocative North Korea has been the PLA. The deep connections between the military leadership in China and in North Korea has really been the mainstay of the relationship. So now all of a sudden new leadership with Xi and his team, and they're saying to the North Koreans—and by extension to the PLA—no. It is not acceptable. We don't need this right now. We've got other things going on. So you're going to have to pull back from your provocative actions, start talking to South Koreans again about the free trade zones, the business zones on the border, and get back to regular order and do it quickly." [Speech to Goldman Sachs, 2013 IBD CEO Annual Conference, 6/4/13]

Hillary Clinton Said She Warned China That If North Korea Continued Developing Its Missile Program, the US Would "Ring China with Missile Defense."

"You know, we all have told the Chinese if they continue to develop this missile program and they get an ICBM that has the capacity to carry a small nuclear weapon on it, which is what they're aiming to do, we cannot abide that. Because they could not only do damage to our treaty allies, namely Japan and South Korea, but they could actually reach Hawaii and the west coast theoretically, and we're going to ring China with missile defense. We're going to put more of our fleet in the area. So China, come on. You either control them or we're going to have to defend against them." [Speech to Goldman Sachs, 2013 IBD CEO Annual Conference, 6/4/13]

China 19

Hillary Clinton Said the Chinese "Have a Right to Assert Themselves" in the South China Sea but the US Needed to "Push Back" so They Don't Get a Chokehold over World Trade.

"48 percent of the world's trade, obviously that includes energy but includes everything else, goes through the South China Sea. Some of you may have seen the long article in the New York Times Magazine on the South China Sea this past weekend, an issue that I worked on for the entire time was in the State Department because China basically wants to control it. You can't hold that against them. They have the right to assert themselves. But if nobody's there to push back to create a balance, then they're going to have a chokehold on the sea lanes and also on the countries that border the South China Sea." [Goldman Sachs Builders and Innovators Summit, 10/29/13]

Hillary Clinton Said She Told the Chinese They Can't Just Claim the South China Sea and by Their Argument the US Could Claim the Pacific Because of World War Two.

"I think that—you know, one of the greatest arguments that I had on a continuing basis was with my Chinese counterparts about their claim. And I made the point at one point in the argument that, you know, you can call it whatever you want to call it. You don't have a claim to all of it. I said, by that argument, you know, the United States should claim all of the Pacific. We liberated it, we defended it. We have as much claim to all of the Pacific. And we could call it the American Sea, and it could go from the West Coast of California all the way to the Philippines. And, you know, my counterpart sat up very straight and goes, well, you can't do that. And I said, well, we have as much right to claim that as you do. I mean, you claim it based on pottery shards from, you know, some fishing vessel that ran aground in an atoll somewhere. You know, we had conveys of military strength. We discovered Japan for Heaven sakes. I mean, we did all of these things." [Goldman Sachs Builders and Innovators Summit, 10/29/13]

Hillary Clinton Said the Chinese Said in That Case They Would Claim Hawaii and She Joked They Would Give China a "Red State."

"MR. BLANKFEIN: These are more technical conversations than I thought they would be. (Laughter.)

SECRETARY CLINTON: Yes, yes. And then he says to me, well, you know, we'll claim Hawaii. And I said, yeah, but we have proof we bought it. Do you have proof you brought any of these places you're claiming? So we got into the nitty-gritty of -

MR. BLANKFEIN: But they have to take New Jersey. (Laughter.)

SECRETARY CLINTON: No, no, no. We're going to give them a red state." [Goldman Sachs Builders and Innovators Summit, 10/29/13]

Hillary Clinton Said the Most Important Advantage the US Has over China Was "Freedom."

"MALE ATTENDEE: Madam Secretary, what is the most important competitive advantage that you think the U.S. will keep as compared to a country like China?

SECRETARY CLINTON: Freedom. I think freedom. Freedom of the mind, freedom of movement, freedom of debate, freedom of innovation. You know, I just—I don't think we fully value—we sometimes take it for granted, and we sometimes even dismiss it, how much stronger we are. Because in addition to that individual freedom that we have in great abundance compared to China, for example, we do have checks and balances. We have constitutional order. We have protection of intellectual property, we have a court system that we use for that purpose. We have a lot of assets that support the free thinking and free acting of individuals. And in the long run, that's what I would place my bet on. I think that is what gives us such a competitive advantage." [Goldman Sachs Builders and Innovators Summit, 10/29/13]

Hillary Clinton Said Freeing Chen Guangchen Was One of Her Proudest Moments as Secretary of State.

"On the opposite end was helping a blind Chinese dissident get safety in the American Embassy in Beijing and then negotiating with the Chinese to get him and his immediate family out of China. That was one of those moments where you have to think hard about what America really stands for so when I got a call late one night saying that Chen Guangcheng had escaped from his house where he had been under house arrest, he'd been picked up by sympathizers and he was on his way to Beijing and he wanted safety in the American Embassy, there were many who said, 'Don't do it, we'll totally destroy our relationship with the Chinese government.' [Jewish United Fund of Metropolitan Chicago Vanguard Luncheon, 10/28/13]

Chapter 7

CLINTON FOUNDATION

Clinton Cited Morocco as a Country Managing Turmoil in the Middle East Well.

"So where are we now? Well, I think let's take them one at a time. Let's take North Africa first, and I won't start with Egypt. I'll start with Morocco. I give King Mohammed the VI a lot of credit for managing a process of change in Morocco. It would be much better to have orderly change that opens up these societies than the kind of terrible carnage we're seeing in Syria and the great confusion and reaction we've seen in Egypt and elsewhere. I don't know what the future holds for Morocco, but that's another country that I would be, you know, advising people to look at and invest in because it seems to have made a transition, at least in this first phase, successfully." [Clinton Speech for General Electric's Global Leadership Meeting—Boca Raton, FL, 1/6/14]

Clinton Thanked BCG for Its Commitment to Clinton Global Initiative during Speech.

"I especially want to thank you for your commitment through the Clinton Global Initiative to educate multi-national manufacturing companies about opportunities for expanding and reshoring operations in the United States." [Clinton Remarks at Boston Consulting Group, 6/20/13]

Clinton Said Canadians, per Capita, Are the Biggest Supporters of the Clinton Foundation.

"Well, I should say thank you because Canadians per capita are the biggest supporters of the Clinton Foundation and the Clinton Global Initiative, so it's great to be supported by so many Canadians." [Remarks at Mediacorp, 11/13/13]

Hillary Clinton Noted Gap Inc. Program's Connection to Clinton Global Initiative.

"I also want to salute your Personal Achievements and Career Enhancement Program known as PACE, P-A-C-E. In partnership with the Clinton Global Initiative that my husband started, PACE has helped more than 14,000 women garment workers in factories in seven countries across Southeast Asia." [Hillary Clinton remarks to Gap Inc., 5/8/13]

Hillary Clinton Thanked Qualcomm for Its Work to Help Women Enter Technology Sector through Clinton Global Initiative Commitments.

HILLARY CLINTON: "Technology, especially mobile technology, has become a crucial tool in promoting participation. That's why we want to see mobile technology in the hands of more people, particularly women and girls. Now, Qualcomm's leadership to this mission has been vital. Your commitments, especially those I would thank you for through the Clinton Global Initiative, are bringing innovative, new approaches to this challenge, like WeTech, which is helping more women and girls get into the technology sector, or your work with the Cherie Blair Foundation to provide online mentoring programs to women in Malaysia, or your Digital Inclusion effort connecting thousands of people in rural Sub-Saharan Africa with communication technology in their own languages." [Hillary Clinton Remarks for Qualcomm, 10/14/14]

Clinton Thanked Bank of America for Its "Exemplary" Work with the Clinton Foundation's Vital Voices.

"Well, let me start with a thank you. I mean, I think Bank of America's partnership with Vital Voices is just exemplary. I mean, what you're doing to support Vital Voices in the mentoring and development arena really matters." [Remarks at Bank of America, 11/13/13]

Hillary Clinton Promoted the Clinton Foundation's Climate Initiative in Delhi, India.

"So a few examples of what we're doing at the Clinton Foundation. First, the Clinton Climate Initiative has a solid waste management program that works with governments and with businesses to reduce their dependency on landfills and develop systems to convert waste into new products or into sources of energy. For example, we are working with the city of Delhi in India to develop that country's first integrated solid waste management system." [Hillary Clinton Remarks at the Institute of Scrap Recycling Industries Convention, 4/10/14]

Hillary Clinton Bragged about the Clinton Climate Initiative Convinced Walmart to Start a Pilot Program on Recycling.

"Now, closer to home the Clinton Climate Initiative wanted to show that recycling can be a better alternative than landfills, even for a huge company like Wal-Mart in a state like Texas, which has, as you know, some of the lightest regulations and lowest landfill costs in the country. So we convinced Walmart to start a pilot program for recycling food waste at three of their superstores in Houston. It has proven to be such a success that the company decided to expand it to every store in the United States that sells groceries, and they're working on taking it global." [Hillary Clinton Remarks at the Institute of Scrap Recycling Industries Convention, 4/10/14]

GIUSTRA, FRANK

Clinton Praised Frank Giustra's Work in Latin America.

"At the Clinton Foundation we have a partnership with Frank Justra (ph), a Canadian businessman, working in Latin America, again focusing on women and their economic agencies, and we used a very old fashioned idea: door-to-door sales in the Andes. We weren't going to bring a big factory or some other large employer but through recruiting dozens at first, then hundreds and maybe eventually thousands of women to be their own employee, their self-employed business, by selling products that would otherwise not be available, we see a ladder of opportunity that had never been created before." [International Leaders' Series, Palais des Congrès de Montréal, 3/18/14]

Chapter 8

CRUZ, TED

Told That Ted Cruz Wanted to Renounce His Canadian Citizenship, Clinton Joked, "Don't Let Him."
FRANK MCKENNA: "And by the way, Teddy Cruz who is one of the apostles or disciples of the Tea Party was born in Canada and wants to renounce his Canadian citizenship. HILLARY CLINTON: Don't let him." FRANK MCKENNA: "Well, there's a lot of us -- a lot of us are prepared to take up a collection if it would help." [Hillary Clinton Remarks at the Vancouver Board of Trade, 3/5/14]

Chapter 9

CUBA

Clinton Described Latin America as Coming out of "Two Good Decades" and Described Countries Were "by and Large" Democratic, except for Cuba.

"That's a great question. You know, I think that we, in America, don't pay enough attention to our neighbors in Latin America. They are our biggest trading partners, bigger than China, bigger than Europe. They have had a good two decades coming out of, in some cases, civil wars, gorilla wars, conflicts, military dictatorships. They are by and large democratic. There are some notable exceptions such as Cuba, but they are have had a good run, and I think there's some adjusting going on in some places right now, but I'm quite optimistic about the entire hemisphere." [Clinton Speech for General Electric's Global Leadership Meeting—Boca Raton, FL, 1/6/14]

Chapter 10

CYBERSECURITY

Clinton Said Issuing an Executive Order on Cybersecurity Would Be in Top Five Executive Order Priorities.

"QUESTION: Hi there. We're had a lot of cyber-attacks this year, Target, Home Depot, JP Morgan, not Deutsche Bank. If you were ever in a position to issue an executive order, where would cyber be in your administration? SEC. HILLARY CLINTON: I think cyber security, cyber warfare are in the top five, because it's a growing threat. And it is a complicated threat to deal with. A lot of the attacks are traced back to either Russia or China, but not exclusively. We've had some Iranian attacks, as some of you know, on distribution of disruption of service in financial institutions. And it's a relatively cheap, labor-intensive way to take advantage of our dependence on the Internet, both for criminal purposes, as well as strategic national purposes." [Clinton Remarks to Deutsche Bank, 10/7/14]

Clinton: "At the State Department We Were Attacked Every Hour, More Than Once an Hour by Incoming Efforts to Penetrate Everything We Had. And That Was True across the US Government."

CLINTON: But, at the State Department we were attacked every hour, more than once an hour by incoming efforts to penetrate everything we had. And that was true across the U.S. government. And we knew it was going on when I would go to China, or I would go to Russia, we would leave all of our electronic equipment on the plane, with the batteries out, because this is a new frontier. And they're trying to find out not just about what we do in our government. They're trying to find out about what a lot of companies do and they were going after the personal emails of people who worked in the State Department. So it's not like the only government in the world that is doing anything is the United States. But, the United States compared to a number of our competitors is the only government in the world with any kind of safeguards, any kind of checks and balances. They may in many respects need to be strengthened and people need to be reassured, and they need to have their protections embodied in law. But, I think turning over a lot of that material intentionally or unintentionally, because of the way it can be drained, gave all kinds of information not only to big countries, but to networks and terrorist groups, and the like. So I have a hard time thinking that somebody who is a champion of privacy and liberty has taken refuge in Russia under Putin's authority. And then he calls into a Putin talk show and says, President Putin, do you spy on people? And President Putin says, well, from one intelligence professional to another, of course not. Oh, thank you so much. I mean, really, I don't know. I have a hard time following it. [Clinton Speech at UConn, 4/23/14]

Cybersecurity 33

***Hillary Clinton: "the State Department Was Attacked Hundreds
of Times Every Day, Some by State-Sponsored Groups, Some by More
Independent Operators."***

"And it's not only on the government side that we should be
worried about. I mean, the cyber-attacks on businesses, and I'm sure
many in this room have experienced that, is aimed at commercial
advantage. In some instances, when it's aimed at defense businesses,
it's aimed at, you know, security and strategic advantage. But, you
know, the State Department was attacked hundreds of times every day,
some by state-sponsored groups, some by more independent operators.
But it was the same effect. People were trying to steal information, use
it for their own purposes." [Goldman Sachs Builders and Innovators
Summit, 10/29/13]

Chapter 11

DEBT LIMIT

Clinton Said the Business View Speaking out during the Debt Limit Debate Was Helpful in Getting through the Crisis.

"So what you saw was a relatively small group in the House of Representatives and very few in the Senate who were trying to achieve one objective, namely make a political point about the health care law by holding hostage the entire rest of the government and putting the full faith in credit of the United States at risk. Although it went up to the last hour, the fact that they were a minority and that there were much more level heads, even in the same political party, that the business view started speaking out after having been relatively silent, thinking this is going to work out, but then people of experience and expertise began speaking out, it was possible to get through that crisis." [Goldman Sachs AIMS Alternative Investments Symposium, 10/24/13]

Chapter 12

EDUCATION

Clinton: Because of the Way Our Education System Is Governed, "Unless You're a Governor or Maybe a Mayor...There's Not Very Much That Most Politicians Can Do."

In her remarks at Knewton, Hillary Clinton said, "I think there have been a number of politicians in the last 35 years, going back to A Nation at Risk, who have been very engaged in and outspoken about education. But unless you're a governor or maybe a mayor who has authority over your schools, there's not really very much that most politicians can do because of the way our system of education is governed. Obviously, local school boards, colleges and universities, they have separate governance. And we don't want politicians interfering too much in the independence of the governance of education. What we want is for politicians to be more knowledgeable about what actually works in education and support that, as opposed to seizing on past ideas and just driving those without regard to evidence." [Hillary Clinton's Remarks at Knewton, 7/22/14]

Hillary Clinton: Common Core Was "A Political Failure."

In her remarks at Knewton, Hillary Clinton said, "The common core is a perfect example. I mean, the common core was negotiated by a bipartisan group of governors. And maybe they thought -- I mean, I think this was a political failure because they negotiated something and they had no real agreed-upon program for explaining it and selling it to people so that they left an opening for those who were always in the education debate, who don't think anybody should be told anything about what to study, even if it's the multiplication tables. You know, that that should all be left to local control. And then you get into more complicated areas, as we all know, that that's just totally off limits. And then using common core results for teacher evaluation when everybody knew that it was going to be complicated to implement." [Hillary Clinton's Remarks at Knewton, 7/22/14]

Chapter 13

EGYPT

Clinton Said after the Egyptian Revolution "We Had to Admit Our Ability to Shape Events Was Highly Limited."

"In our foreign policy that means, among other things, getting good at balancing our long-term interests against short-term pressures. That's what we tried to do when the revolution broke out in Egypt. And the National Security Team gathered around the table in the situation room day after day facing a difficult set of choices. First of all, we had to admit our ability to shape events was highly limited. The Mubarak Regime had refused to reform despite our warnings over years and was crumbling in the face of widespread popular protest. Egyptian citizens were, after all, demanding the chance to shape their own destinies. On the one hand this was encouraging. We believe in democracy, not just on moral and philosophical grounds, but because over the long run, democracy gives us more partners and fewer adversaries. But let's be honest. Mubarak had been an ally of the United States for many years. We have important interests in the region in addition to democracy including our fight against terrorism; defense of our allies, especially Israel; and a secure supply of energy. There are times in government, as

40 *Christian Mellor*

in business, when not all of our interests align. Now, we work to align them, but that's just the reality." [Clinton Speech for Morgan Stanley, 4/18/13]

Clinton: "The Muslim Brotherhood Won. In The Beginning We Said They Won Legitimately. We Worked With Them."

"But, I have to say I was not convincing. I did not persuade the young people to do that and you know what happened. The Muslim Brotherhood won. In the beginning we said they won legitimately. We worked with them. We tried to persuade them, starting with President Morsi, to run an inclusive government, to make every Egyptian feel that they had a place at the table. They became much more interested in promoting their ideology that produced a reaction. The military took over and now a general has become president. So those were very hard decisions to try to figure out how to manage on all of these fronts. But, the point I hope you take away is change for the sake of change is not going to make the difference you hope for unless you are prepared and organized to follow up on that change and politics, small P politics, is the way people in democracies work together to try to institutionalize the changes that you are seeking and I don't know if we're going to see any renewal of that kind of hopefulness in the Arab world for quite some time, because of the problems that arose as a result of overthrowing existing regimes without anything to fill the vacuum." [Remarks to Fundacion TelMex, 9/5/14]

Hillary Clinton Said Egypt Posed a Threat to the Israelis Due to the Unpredictability of the Morsi Government, and to the Saudis and Emiratis Because Their Version of Political Islam Was a Threat to Their Status Quo.

"Certainly Egypt posed very direct threats to Israel because of the, number one, instability and then number two, the unpredictability of the Morsi government. That also posed in the eyes of the Saudis and

Egypt   41

the Emiratis a threat to them because they view the organized efforts for political Islam to be threatening their status quo. We also were very concerned about the breeding of instability in terrorist havens in the Sinai which could be used just as the FATA between Pakistan and Afghanistan had been used by Al-Qaeda as launching sites for extremist attacks against Egypt, against Israel, against Jordan and further afield in the Gulf." [Jewish United Fund of Metropolitan Chicago Vanguard Luncheon, 10/28/13]

Hillary Clinton Said Mubarak Prevented the Formation of Any Opposition, Which Made the Muslim Brotherhood the Only Organized Opposition When His Regime Fell.

"Well, I am one who was very cautious about the aftereffects of the Arab Spring, in part because there was no organized opposition that was not the Muslim Brotherhood. What Mubarak had done, unfortunately, for more than 30 years was to really prevent any other outlets for political positions, for any letting off of steam, any organization of groups that had policy or political goals. And the Muslim Brotherhood, despite Mubarak's best efforts to try to break it, was able to continue to develop because it had the mosques, and it had small businesses. And it had a network that he could never penetrate, but the non-Islamic opposition was decimated." [2014 Jewish United Fund Advance & Major Gifts Dinner, 10/28/13]

Hillary Clinton Said She Went to Egypt after the Uprising and Found the Opposition to Be "Political Neophytes to the Nth Degree."

"So after Tahrir Square, I went to Egypt to see what was going on. That was before the presidential election had been held; it was still while the military was in charge trying to figure out how to run presidential elections. And I met with representatives of a lot of the groups that had been at Tahrir Square with all of their optimism and enthusiasm and their inclusivity between Muslims and Christian Copts and all the

Twittering and Facebooking that they were doing, and they were political neophytes to the nth degree." [2014 Jewish United Fund Advance & Major Gifts Dinner, 10/28/13]

Hillary Clinton Said Her Meetings with the Political Opposition Left Her Pessimistic about Their Ability to Be an Opposition for the Muslim Brotherhood.

"They had no experience, no understanding about how to organize political parties, how to run candidates, how to conduct campaigns. They didn't have platforms. They were totally divided, and I came away feeling very pessimistic that there could be a vigorous opposition to the Muslim Brotherhood. And yet at the same time, holding elections is something we favor in our country, and we believe that elections are not in and of themselves sufficient because too many people believe in one election one time and then they never give up power. So we tried hard to continue to work to build up a secular opposition." [2014 Jewish United Fund Advance & Major Gifts Dinner, 10/28/13]

Hillary Clinton Said the US Couldn't Not Support an Election in Egypt but Eventually Morsi's Government Became "More Authoritarian," Which Caused His Removal.

"So it put the United States, it put Europeans, it put everybody in a difficult position because you can't say you are for democracy and not support democratic aspirations, something that the United States governments have been pushing Egypt to do for decades, both Republican and Democratic administrations, and you have to try to do everything you can to influence, in a democratic way, those who win. Upshot was that as time went by, it became more and more apparent, first and foremost to Egyptians that the Morsi government was becoming more authoritarian, much less open, and that caused, as we

Egypt 43

saw, the upheaval leading to his removal." [2014 Jewish United Fund Advance & Major Gifts Dinner, 10/28/13]

Hillary Clinton Said Morsi Was Very Naïve about Al-Qaeda and Extremism.

So he came into office quite naive. I remember one of my very first meetings with him saying 'What are you going to do to prevent Al-Qaeda and other extremists from taking up positions inside Egypt and, in particular, in the Sinai?' His response was, 'Well, why would they do that? We have an Islamist government now. Why would they do that?' And I said, 'Because you will never be pure enough. It does not matter. I don't care what your positions are. You cannot be a president of a country and not do everything you can to protect your country against these internal threats.'" [2014 Jewish United Fund Advance & Major Gifts Dinner, 10/28/13]

Hillary Clinton Said What Happened in Egypt Was a "Military Takeover" and No One Was Willing to "Make the Hard Reform Necessary for the Economy."

"We are kind of back to the future. We have a military takeover. We have a planned-for election, likely winner to be one of the generals, if not al-Sisi himself, and we have a lot of continuing instability and violence within Egypt and a deteriorating economy because neither of the Morsi government nor the military leadership is willing to make the hard reform necessary for the economy to be stabilized and grow in a way to meet the needs of the Egyptian people." [2014 Jewish United Fund Advance & Major Gifts Dinner, 10/28/13]

Hillary Clinton Implied That America Was "Pretty Close" to Doing Nothing in Egypt and That No One Likes the US There at the Moment.

"MR. LESTER CROWN: Do we then have actually three choices: Either military, Muslim Brotherhood or do nothing? Under those circumstances, should we have suspended aid to the one who was at least the least bad of those three? Because we really can't do nothing. Egypt is tremendously important to the region, to us, to Israel, to everything else. So doing nothing is really not an option. MS. HILLARY CLINTON: Well, there are some who would argue that's pretty close to what we're doing because we put into—I say we, the Administration, was put into a very difficult position and I think did all that it could under our own laws to not be pushed into taking action that could sever the relationship that we had built up over the years since the Camp David Accords with the Egyptian military. Nobody likes us in Egypt right now. It doesn't matter whether you are on the military side, the Muslim Brotherhood side, the young blogger side. Everybody thinks we supported the other guy, and what I believe the Administration tried to do was to support principles and values and keep pressure on the Muslim Brotherhood and others to try to move toward actions that would be much more democratically recognizable, embedded in the Egyptian government and society." [2014 Jewish United Fund Advance & Major Gifts Dinner, 10/28/13]

Hillary Clinton Said the Military Would Govern Egypt for as Long as They Wanted and Were Being Supported by the Saudis and Emiratis.

"So it's, right now, playing itself out. The military is going to remain in charge for as long as they choose to, really. They are going to face more internal threats that they are going to have to be very tough in dealing with, and they are going to try to, in as much as they can, squash the Muslim Brotherhood and their political arm. And they are getting a lot of help from the Saudis to the Emiratis—to go back to our original discussion—because the Saudis and the Emiratis see the Muslim Brotherhood as threatening to them, which is kind of ironic since the Saudis have exported more extreme ideology than any other place on earth over the course of the last 30 years." [2014 Jewish United Fund Advance & Major Gifts Dinner, 10/28/13]

Egypt 45

Hillary Clinton Said the Saudis Opposed the Muslim Brotherhood, "Which Is Kind of Ironic since the Saudis Have Exported More Extreme Ideology Than Any Other Place on Earth over the Course of the Last 30 Years."

"And they are getting a lot of help from the Saudis to the Emiratis—to go back to our original discussion—because the Saudis and the Emiratis see the Muslim Brotherhood as threatening to them, which is kind of ironic since the Saudis have exported more extreme ideology than any other place on earth over the course of the last 30 years." [2014 Jewish United Fund Advance & Major Gifts Dinner, 10/28/13]

Hillary Clinton Said the US and Israel Would Need to Continue Working the Egyptian Military, "but Egypt Is Going to Go through Its Own Turmoil for a While."

"But they see the current situation as one that they have to help the Egyptian military manage and control. So it's not that we take a position of doing nothing. It's that right now we are continuing most of the aid to the Egyptian military. We are continuing the kind of ongoing contacts that we've done for decades. We are working with the Israelis who are reestablishing their connections and on an ongoing, consultative basis working to keep the Sinai under control and try to head off other threats. But Egypt is going to go through its own turmoil for a while, and they need a leader and a leadership ethos that will actually try and improve the lives of Egyptian people." [2014 Jewish United Fund Advance & Major Gifts Dinner, 10/28/13]

Hillary Clinton: "I Mean the Biggest Rebuke to Mubarak Is That He Was in Power for More Than 30 Years and in Many Ways the Country Was Worse off When He Left Than When He Came."

"I mean the biggest rebuke to Mubarak is that he was in power for more than 30 years and in many ways the country was worse off when he left than when he came on literacy, on health, on all kinds of indicators, and the jobs for educated Egyptians are few and far between and on and on." [2014 Jewish United Fund Advance & Major Gifts Dinner, 10/28/13]

Chapter 14

EQUAL PAY

When Asked What Needed to Change to Close the Pay Gap, Clinton Said We Needed to Enforce the Laws Already on the Books.

"MS. TINKHAM: Okay. What about the wage gap? So the U.S. Census Bureau released data recently that in 2012, women still earned only 77 cents to every dollar on men. What do you think needs to change to make that more even? SECRETARY CLINTON: Well, I think we have laws on the books. Enforcing them is the first step. And too often it is very difficult for the woman who herself is being discriminated against. You know, the Lilly Ledbetter case which established firmly the absolute right to be paid equally for equal work was a great step forward, but if people don't know about it, if they don't have a safe harbor to go to get somebody to advocate for them, you know, it's not going to increase the number of women being paid what they should be paid. So I think first and foremost, we have to enforce the law." [Accenture Women's Leadership Forum, 10/24/13]

Chapter 15

EMAIL

Hillary Clinton: "When I Got to the State Department, It Was Still against the Rules to Let Most—or Let All Foreign Service Officers Have Access to a Blackberry."

"I mean, let's face it, our government is woefully, woefully behind in all of its policies that affect the use of technology. When I got to the State Department, it was still against the rules to let most—or let all Foreign Service Officers have access to a Blackberry. You couldn't have desktop computers when Colin Powell was there. Everything that you are taking advantage of, inventing and using, is still a generation or two behind when it comes to our government." [Hillary Clinton Remarks at Nexenta, 8/28/14]

Hillary Clinton: "We Couldn't Take Our Computers, We Couldn't Take Our Personal Devices" off the Plane in China and Russia.

"I mean, probably the most frustrating part of this whole debate are countries acting like we're the only people in the world trying to figure out what's going on. I mean, every time I went to countries like China or Russia, I mean, we couldn't take our computers, we couldn't take our personal devices, we couldn't take anything off the plane because they're so good, they would penetrate them in a minute, less, a nanosecond. So we would take the batteries out, we'd leave them on the plane." [Hillary Clinton Remarks at Nexenta, 8/28/14]

Clinton Said When She Got to State, Employees "Were Not Mostly Permitted to Have Handheld Devices."

"You know, when Colin Powell showed up as Secretary of State in 2001, most State Department employees still didn't even have computers on their desks. When I got there they were not mostly permitted to have handheld devices. I mean, so you're thinking how do we operate in this new environment dominated by technology, globalizing forces? We have to change, and I can't expect people to change if I don't try to model it and lead it." [Clinton Speech for General Electric's Global Leadership Meeting – Boca Raton, FL, 1/6/14]

Hillary Clinton Said You Know You Can't Bring Your Phone and Computer When Traveling to China and Russia and She Had to Take Her Batteries out and Put Them in a Special Box.

"And anybody who has ever traveled in other countries, some of which shall remain nameless, except for Russia and China, you know that you can't bring your phones and your computers. And if you do, good luck. I mean, we would not only take the batteries out, we would leave the batteries and the devices on the plane in special boxes. Now, we didn't do that because we thought it would be fun to tell somebody about. We did it because we knew that we were all targets and that we would be totally vulnerable. So it's not only what others do to us and what we do to them and how many people are involved in it. It's what's the purpose of it, what is being collected, and how can it be used. And there are clearly people in this room who know a lot about this, and some of you could be very useful contributors to that conversation because you're sophisticated enough to know that it's not just, do it, don't do it. We have to have a way of doing it, and then we have to have a way of analyzing it, and then we have to have a way of sharing it." [Goldman Sachs Builders and Innovators Summit, 10/29/13]

Hillary Clinton Lamented How Far behind the State Department Was in Technology, Saying "People Were Not Even Allowed to Use Mobile Devices Because of Security Issues."

"Personally, having, you know, lived and worked in the White House, having been a senator, having been Secretary of State, there has traditionally been a great pool of very talented, hard-working people. And just as I was saying about the credit market, our personnel policies haven't kept up with the changes necessary in government. We have a lot of difficulties in getting—when I got to the State Department, we were so far behind in technology, it was embarrassing. And, you know, people were not even allowed to use mobile devices because of security issues and cost issues, and we really had to try to push into the last part of the 20th Century in order to get people functioning in 2009 and '10." [Goldman Sachs Builders and Innovators Summit, 10/29/13]

Hillary Clinton Noted Snowden Traveled with Sensitive Material on Computers and Asked "Why Are Those Computers Not Exploited When My Cellphone Was Going to Be Exploited?"

"I can't speak one way or the other on that. But what I think is true, despite Snowden's denials, is that if he actually showed up in Hong Kong with computers and then showed up in Mexico with computers, why are those computers not exploited when my cellphone was going to be exploited." [Goldman Sachs Builders and Innovators Summit, 10/29/13]

Chapter 16

EMANUEL, RAHM

Clinton Encouraged Attendees of the ASCP Annual Meeting in Chicago to "Spend Some Money, Because [Emanuel] Probably Has Surveillance Watching to Determine Who Does and Doesn't."

"Thank you so much. I'm deeply honored to receive this award from such an esteemed organization. I know that the mayor is rushing off to his next assigned event and responsibility. I just want to thank him and tell you that reliving a lot of my experiences with Rahm makes me once again realize how much you want him in any foxhole you end up in, maybe not at Buckingham Palace for tea with the Queen, but for any other challenging situation, he always had my back. He always had both President Clinton's and President Obama's back, and now he's got Chicago's back. So if I were you, I would find some way to go spend some money because he probably has surveillance watching to determine who does and who doesn't." [American Society for Clinical Pathology Annual Meeting, 9/18/13]

Clinton Praised Rahm Emanuel for "Working Very Hard to Try to Get a Handle on What Is a Terrible Blight of Gun Violence in Chicago."

"Well, first of all, I think there's two parts to this. One is Chicago in particular and I know that Mayor Emanuel and the government of Chicago and a lot of the partners in the community throughout Chicago are working very hard to try to get a handle on what is a terrible blight of gun violence in Chicago." [Chicago House Remarks, 9/18/13]

Clinton: Rahm Emanuel Is "Working to Come up with the Solutions That Really Fit Whatever the Problems in Chicago Are."

"On the first issue, you know, I know from having talked with Rahm about this that he is, you know, working to come up with the solutions that really fit whatever the problems in Chicago are. I mean, I can remember a long time ago knowing that gang violence in Chicago was particularly dangerous, and it's only gotten more so because of the Mexican drug cartels and others who have roots going to Chicago as distribution points throughout the Midwest. So every situation has to be analyzed, but there are some general criteria. You do need enough police on the streets, and that is something that communities are now facing because of the cutbacks, the sequestrations and other budget pressures." [Chicago House Remarks, 9/18/13]

Clinton: "I Know Chicago Is Working. It Has to Be a Whole-Of-Government, Really a Whole-Of-City Approach."

"I remember, you know, when Bill ran for President and he talked a lot about community policing, he said that, you know, in 1960, there were three police for every felon, and by 1990, we had three felons for every police officer. So manpower does make a difference. Equally, strong, positive partnerships with community groups and leaders makes a difference particularly to intervene and try to prevent young people from getting sucked into gangs or being enticed into violence because of their need to feel part of something. So I know Chicago is working.

It has to be a whole-of-government, really a whole-of-city approach." [Chicago House Remarks, 9/18/13]

At A Speech To A Jewish Group In Chicago, Hillary Clinton Said "Rahm And I Were Talking Backstage About What He's Trying To Do Here In The City For Preschool And After School And Jobs For Unemployed Young People." "So one of the great challenges as we look at our trend lines, our social and cultural trend lines, is to begin to focus where our efforts can make the most difference, where we can begin to try to reverse some of the changes that are not in America's interests. Now, for me, that starts with our children. Rahm and I were talking backstage about what he's trying to do here in the city for preschool and after school and jobs for unemployed young people. I feel strongly that these kinds of efforts are needed now more than ever, and maybe it's harder to summon the political will and to find the scarce resources, but just as we did during the Great Depression by giving people a sense that they still had meaning and purpose and would be part of the new future in America, we have to look seriously at what is happening among our youngest children." [Jewish United Fund of Metropolitan Chicago Vanguard Luncheon, 10/28/13]

Hillary Clinton Praised Mitch Landrieu and Rahm Emanuel as Mayors Doing Good Work.

"SECRETARY CLINTON: Well, look, I—I think that everyone agrees that we're in a bad patch in our political system and in Washington. It's—you know, there's a lot of good things happening elsewhere in the country. There are a lot of mayors, you had Mitch Landrieu here, I was with Rahm Emanuel yesterday. There's a lot of innovative, interesting, new ideas being put into practice by mayors, by some governors. So I think when we talk about our political system, we're really focusing more on what's happening in Washington. And it is dysfunctional right now. And it is for a variety of reasons, some of them systemic, as you suggested." [Goldman Sachs Builders and Innovators Summit, 10/29/13]

Chapter 17

ENERGY

CONTINUING TO USE FOSSIL FUELS

Clinton: "Of Course, We're Going to Continue Using Fossil Fuels, but I Think We Should Set the Global Example for Transitioning in Some More Orderly Way Away from Fossil Fuels..."

"We could do so much more. Looking across North America at our electric grids, you know we have coal-fired plants in the United States that went online when Franklin Roosevelt was President. That can't possibly be smart. And what President Obama did with the EPA rules to begin to try to lower greenhouse gas emissions primarily from burning coal is an important step that shouldn't be seen in isolation. It should be seen as part of a broader energy strategy. Of course, we're going to continue using fossil fuels, but I think we should set the global example for transitioning in some more orderly way away from fossil fuels, and given the innovation, given the research capacity, given the experiences on both sides of our border, we're in a perfect position to do that." [Remarks at tinePublic, 6/18/14]

DOMESTIC GAS PRODUCTION

Hillary Clinton Noted the Unlocking of Gas from Shale Formations as an Advance in Technology.

"The unlocking of, you know, gas from shale formations, the advances in technology that have improved our ability to go back to what we thought were dry wells and drill for oil." [05162013 Remarks to Banco Itau.doc, p. 34]

Hillary Clinton Said the Transition from Coal to Natural Gas Has Contributed to the Economic Recovery.

"It's one of the contributing factors to our economic recovery and to at least the, you know, the resumption of manufacturing because of the lower prices for natural gas and cleaning up to some limited extent emissions because of the transfer from coal to natural gas." [05162013 Remarks to Banco Itau.doc, p. 35]

Hillary Clinton Said the United States Has an Opportunity to Be an Energy Exporter.

"It will certainly make us less dependent on Middle East oil or on Venezuelan oil over time, which I think gives us an opportunity not only to take care of our own needs but to be an exporter, you know, in the market." [05162013 Remarks to Banco Itau.doc, p. 35]

Hillary Clinton Said She's Not Crazy about the Consequences of Natural Gas—with the Release of Methane—but It Is Replacing Coal.

"Secondly we do have to work on diminishing our reliance on fossil fuels but there's going to be bridging there, there's no alternative especially in other countries. I'm not crazy about the consequences of natural gas with the release of methane but it is replacing coal. We have to be smarter about the technology and about the control of how we extract oil and gas in the United States and elsewhere to try to get as close to a clean bridge as possible." [02262014 HWA Remarks at UMiami.DOC, p. 24]

Hillary Clinton Said Advances in Technology Have Enabled the Capture of Oil and Gas, Including Hydraulic Fracturing.

"And the advances in technology that have enabled the capture of oil and gas in -- you know, from hydraulic fracturing and other approaches that was just not possible a decade or two ago has created this enormous opportunity for us." [02042014 HWA Remarks at Citi [Westchester].DOC, p. 24]

Hillary Clinton Said We Have to Figure Out If We're Going to Export Energy Sources, and That's a Complicated Issue.

Third, we have to figure out if we're going to export. And that's a complicated issue and sides are being drawn and you have some arguing that we should not export, at least not for the foreseeable future; that we should try to lower the cost of energy in this country, we should try to replace as much coal as possible, we should try to use clean energy, namely natural gas for more transportation, more manufacturing, and that should be our first priority before we get to any kind of export regime. Obviously, on the other side, led principally by the gas and oil industry, they want to, you know, begin exporting, building the refineries, getting into the business. [02042014 HWA Remarks at Citi [Westchester].DOC, pg. 25]

Hillary Clinton Said the Federal Government, through the Department of Energy, Pioneered Hydraulic Fracturing and Has an Obligation to Help Develop Regulations.

"And the federal government which, basically, through the Department of Energy, pioneered hydraulic fracturing, has an obligation to work with states to come up with those kinds of regulations. You know, we've got to make sure that we're not releasing methane in the air. That's a great house gas, that's not a good outcome.

60 *Christian Mellor*

We have to be sure that, you know, we are protecting the water supply. We have to, you know, make it possible for local communities to have some greater knowledge about the chemicals that are used." [02042014 HWA Remarks at Citi [Westchester].DOC, p. 24]

Clinton Said She Wanted the US and Canada to Work toward Finding Opportunities Energy Independence, as New Techniques for Extracting Oil and Gas Emerged.

"But looking at Canada and the United States, I personally would like to see a process bringing together decision-makers, experts, in looking at where we could have greater symmetry between our electric grids, our gas and oil, because what is happening, as you know so well, Frank, is that with the new discoveries, with the new techniques for extracting oil and gas, the United States and Canada are going to be powerhouses for however the gas is transported and used or exported. We have tremendous opportunities now to be energy independent, energy secure, and that has great ramifications for our own economies and societies as well as globally." [Hillary Clinton Remarks at the Vancouver Board of Trade, 3/5/14]

Hillary Clinton Praised American and Canadian Leadership Towards Energy Independence.

"Our friends in the Caribbean pay the highest prices for electricity in the world, with a combination of geography and oligarchy that had prevented those countries from moving towards energy affordability and independence. Now, one of the reasons I'm optimistic about the future of the Americas is because this hemisphere can really be the anchor for peace, progress and prosperity for the entire world. If one thinks about the diversity and the democratization and the progress that has been made in North and Central and South America, it is mind-boggling. When it comes to energy, global competitiveness, leadership on the world stage and so much else, our hemisphere is positioned to

Energy 61

thrive, led by North America, if we work together." [Canada 2020 Speech, 10/6/14]

Hillary Clinton Noted That Domestic Oil and Gas Production Were Set to Surpass Russia.

"I've dealt with him over a number of years. He is a very tough customer. He has a lot of problems inside Russia, you know, they're much too dependent on oil and gas, and with all of our oil and gas discoveries and production in the United States, we are in a path to surpass Russia in actual oil and gas production. I hope we know what we're doing to take advantage of that, but he's used Russian resources to really intimidate his neighbors." [LIA Speech, 10/4/13]

Clinton Said She Wanted the United States to Export Gas.

"Right now, we have a platform for increasing manufacturing, for decreasing the cost of energy that I don't want to lose, but at the same time I want to be able to export gas, especially to our friends, in order to undercut in Europe's case the pressure from Russia, or in Asia's case the turn back to using Iran if we don't figure out a way to resolve our nuclear issue." [Clinton Remarks to Deutsche Bank, 10/7/14]

Hillary Clinton Praised the Increase in Gas and Oil Production in the US, Saying "We Are Now Energy Independent, Something We Have Hoped for and Worked for over Many, Many Years."

In her remarks at Ameriprise, Hillary Clinton said, "And as we speak, Gazprom is attempting to take over other strategic energy infrastructure in Europe. This is pure power politics. And that's why as secretary of state, starting in March of 2009, I pushed the Europeans to get serious about finding alternative energy sources, and to invest real resources in their infrastructure so they would not be at Putin's mercy. [...] And we're in such a great position to do that because of the increase in gas and oil production in our own country, we are now energy independent, something we have hoped for and worked for over many, many years. That gives us tools we didn't have before. And it also gives us the opportunity not only to invest those resources in more manufacturing and other activities that benefit us directly here at home, but to be a bulwark with our supplies against the kind of intimidation we see going on from Russia." [Hillary Clinton's Remarks at Ameriprise, 7/26/14]

Hillary Clinton Called Increased Oil and Gas Production in the US a "Tremendous Opportunity," but Said It Needed to Be Extracted in a Way That Would Not Harm the Environment.

In remarks at Robbins, Gellar, Rudman & Dowd in San Diego, Hillary Clinton said, "I'll make a couple of points, because it's really an important question. Number one, because of changes in technology as all of you know, we are now producing more oil and gas than we ever have in our history and we're on our way to be the number one producer in the world. Now, that is a tremendous opportunity, as long as we are smart about it. And we have to start by being smart about making sure we extract oil and gas in ways that don't destroy water tables, leak methane into the air, undermine the quality of life for people who live near the wells. And we have to do that. And there will be some places, frankly, where we will have to decide we can't do it there. But, many places we'll be able to, as long as we have the appropriate precautions undertaken." [Hillary Clinton's Remarks at Robbins Geller Rudman & Dowd in San Diego, 9/04/14]

Hillary Clinton: I Favor Oil and Gas Exports "under the Appropriate Circumstances."

In remarks at Robbins, Gellar, Rudman & Dowd in San Diego, Hillary Clinton said, "Secondly, then we have to decide are we going to start exporting? And after the era of embargo back in '73 we stopped. We don't export, because we didn't have enough for ourselves and we didn't want to be giving it away. But, now we have to be, again, smart about trying to figure out how much we can export, what are the

Energy 63

triggers for stopping exporting, natural disasters, other kinds of challenges that maybe we export, but we can always shut it off and everybody in the industry knows that, in the event of certain on certain consequences that we have to deal with. I favor going into exporting under the appropriate circumstances and I'll be saying in my remarks later today that exporting to Europe would really weaken Putin's hand, which is very important, because I think otherwise he's not going to be stopped. We have to call him up short, and that's the best way and then just demanding that the Europeans do more for themselves." [Hillary Clinton's Remarks at Robbins Geller Rudman & Dowd in San Diego, 9/04/14]

Hillary Clinton: "The Energy Revolution in the United States is Just a Gift, and We're Able to Exploit It and Use It and It's Going to Make Us Independent."

"We were talking at dinner. I mean, the energy revolution in the United States is just a gift, and we're able to exploit it and use it and it's going to make us independent. We can have a North American energy system that will be unbelievably powerful. If we have enough of it we can be exporting and supporting a lot of our friends and allies. "[Speech to Goldman Sachs, 2013 IBD CEO Annual Conference, 6/4/13]

Hillary Clinton: "I Think It's Mostly a Positive That We Are More Energy Sufficient. Obviously It's Imperative That We Exploit the Oil and Gas in the Most Environmentally Careful Way Because We Don't Want to—We Don't Want to Cause Problems."

"SECRETARY CLINTON: Well, look, I think it's mostly, again, on the balance sheet metaphor of where we are in the world today. I think it's mostly a positive that we are more energy sufficient. Obviously it's imperative that we exploit the oil and gas in the most environmentally careful way because we don't want to—we don't want to cause problems that we also will have to deal with taking advantage

of what is a quite good windfall for us in many other respects."
[Goldman Sachs Builders and Innovators Summit, 10/29/13]

Clinton: "So I Think That Keystone Is a Contentious Issue, and of Course It Is Important on Both Sides of the Border for Different and Sometimes Opposing Reasons..."

"So I think that Keystone is a contentious issue, and of course it is important on both sides of the border for different and sometimes opposing reasons, but that is not our relationship. And I think our relationship will get deeper and stronger and put us in a position to really be global leaders in energy and climate change if we worked more closely together. And that's what I would like to see us do."
[Remarks at tinePublic, 6/18/14]

NUCLEAR POWER

Clinton: "Nuclear Deserves a Role. The Problem with Nuclear Is That It Is Just Not Economically Feasible for Private Interests to Build Nuclear Plants, at Least in Our Country."

"I think that we have to be looking to try to do more on the clean energy side even as we continue on the fossil fuel side. We already have dozens of pipelines crossing our borders, you all know that. And we have hundreds of tankers on trains crossing our borders. So it's not like one pipeline is going to make the difference between the trading in fossil fuels between our two countries, but I think that there are other ways we could be smarter about how to change our energy mix, and to provide the right incentives to do that. Nuclear deserves a role. The problem with nuclear is that it is just not economically feasible for private interests to build nuclear plants, at least in our country. The cost, the liabilities are so enormous. Well, are there second, third, fourth, fifth generation nuclear reactors that would be less expensive, more

Energy 65

efficient, cheaper, not cheaper but more safe, safer. We should have a Manhattan Project about all of this, to coin a description from a previous era that opened the nuclear age." [Remarks for CIBC, 1/22/15]

PROMOTING FRACKING GLOBALLY

Hillary Clinton Praised Argentina for Using New Technologies to Unlock Natural Gas.

"The United States is not the only country in our hemisphere enjoying an energy revolution, Canada, Mexico, Brazil, is developing major new oil finds, continues to lead the way on bio fuels. Argentina is using new technologies to unlock natural gas." [05162013 Remarks to Banco Itau.doc, p. 19]

Clinton: "The Whole Idea of How Fracking Came to Be Available in the Marketplace is Because of Research Done by Our Government. And I've Promoted Fracking in Other Places around the World."

CLINTON: So I am an all-in kind of person, all-of-the-above kind of person when it comes to America's energy and environmental future. And I would like us to get over the political divide and put our heads together and figure out how we can be really, really smart about doing this. I mean, fracking was developed at the Department of Energy. I mean, the whole idea of how fracking came to be available in the marketplace is because of research done by our government. And I've promoted fracking in other places around the world. Because when you look at the strangle-hold that energy has on so many countries and the decisions that they make, it would be in America's interest to make even more countries more energy self-sufficient. So I think we have to go at this in a smart, environmentally conscious way, pursuing a clean-energy alternative agenda while we also promote the advantages that are going to come to us, especially in manufacturing, because we're now going to

66 *Christian Mellor*

produce more oil and gas. And that's what I would like to see us talking about instead of standing on two sides of the divide and not working to try to minimize the damage and maximize the upside. [Clinton Speech for Deutsche Bank, 4/24/13]

Clinton: "With the New Technology Known as Fracking, We Are Truly on a Path—and It's Not Just United States; It's All of North America—That Will Be Net Energy Exporters Assuming We Do It Right."

AUDIENCE MEMBER: Thanks very much. I'm wondering if you can comment on the issues at stake in the evaluation of the Keystone XL pipeline and maybe more broadly talk about the role that energy and the environment both play in our foreign policy. SECRETARY CLINTON: Well, I can talk generally. I can't specifically, because the State Department makes the decision, recommendation about Keystone pipeline, and it's not appropriate for me to comment on the merits or on the ultimate decision. But it is something that I care deeply about, energy and the environment, because I think we have a fabulous opportunity to get both right in this country. As Secretary of State I created the first Energy Bureau, because, as you know, we're on the cusp of being energy self-sufficient. And that is a big change from where we were a decade ago. The ability to extract both gas and oil from previously used places that didn't seem to have much more to offer, but now the technology gives us the chance to go in and recover oil and gas; or with the new technology known as fracking, we are truly on a path—and it's not just United States; it's all of North America—that will be net energy exporters assuming we do it right. And doing it right means not sacrificing the environment in ways that are preventable. There will always be some environmental cost in extracting hydrocarbons, rare earth minerals, you name it from both the earth and the oceans. But we ought to be smart enough, and we ought to be committed enough to ensure that we set the example for the world about how to do it with the minimal amount of environmental

Energy 67

damage. I think that's all within our reach. And I believe that we can afford to do it, and I think we have an obligation to do it. So I want to see us become the number one oil and gas producer while we also pursue a clean-energy agenda at the same time. I don't think it has to be either or. I think it's a mistake to think it does. I happen to think we are missing a great opportunity by not dealing with climate change, not just because it's a rolling crisis that we're dealing with, but also I think there's a lot of money to be made from pioneering and manufacturing and exporting and creating a global market for how we deal with climate change. [Clinton Speech for Deutsche Bank, 4/24/13]

Clinton Talked about "Phony Environmental Groups" Funded by the Russians to Stand against Pipelines and Fracking.

"We were up against Russia pushing oligarchs and others to buy media. We were even up against phony environmental groups, and I'm a big environmentalist, but these were funded by the Russians to stand against any effort, oh that pipeline, that fracking that whatever will be a problem for you, and a lot of the money supporting that message was coming from Russia." [Remarks at tinePublic, 6/18/14]

Clinton Discussed Promoting Oil Pipelines and Fracking in Eastern Europe.

"So how far this aggressiveness goes I think is really up to us. I would like to see us accelerating the development of pipelines from Azerbaijan up into Europe. I would like to see us looking for ways to accelerate the internal domestic production. Poland recently signed a big contract to explore hydraulic fracturing to see what it could produce. Apparently, there is thought to be some good reserves there. And just really go at this in a self-interested, smart way. The Russians can only intimidate you if you are dependent upon them." [International Leaders' Series, Palais des Congrès de Montréal, 3/18/14]

Hillary Clinton Began Urging Europe to Be More Energy Independent and Pushing for "a More Competitive Marketplace for Energy."

"HILLARY CLINTON: [On Putin] Secondly, the effort to undermine the market in oil and gas and commodities goes right at the source of Russia's wealth. When I was Secretary I cannot say I saw this coming, but what I saw was that in 2006 in January he cut off gas to Eastern Europe. I think like a dozen people froze to death in Poland. He did it again in 2009, primarily focused on Ukraine. He has used his energy weapon to intimidate Europe. And starting in 2009 I began having conversations with the Europeans that they had to do more to be more independent and to push for a more competitive marketplace for energy. I formed something called the U.S.-EU Energy Council and began trying to look at what more we could do to really wean people away from Russian supplies. The more we can do that the more difficult it will be for Putin to maintain his hold on leadership, even with his inner circle without changing course." [Hillary Clinton Remarks at Marketo, 4/8/14]

REDUCING EMISSIONS

Clinton Said That China and India's Initial Reluctance to Reduce Emissions Was a "Totally Rational Response If You Were the Leader of China or India."

"And at that time you could not get China and India to agree to do anything on their emissions because they, I think understandably, one an authoritarian regime, one a democracy, a raucous democracy, were of the opinion it would interfere with their efforts to continue to grow, a totally rational response if you were the leader of China or India." [Remarks for CIBC, 1/22/15]

Energy 69

Hillary Clinton Talked up Her Work on Clean Cookstoves to Fight Climate Change.

"One quick example. One of the biggest contributors to climate change are the short-acting pollutants, methane and black carbon, soot as we sometimes call it. One of the biggest contributors to that are cook stoves, you know, more than a billion-plus women and girls every day cooking on fires, burning not just wood but dung and other kinds of material. And so it became clear that if we could create a market for a different kind of cook stove, we would accomplish not only a drop in the contributors to climate change that flow from that but also save lives because the fourth-leading cause of death now in the entire world are respiratory ailments due to women and mostly girls cooking over these stoves, very often inside small contained places during cold weather, but even without being in climates that change, having that kind of responsibility hour after hour, day after day, has serious health consequences. So we put together an international alliance for clean cook stoves, and we worked of course with governments but we also began working with the private sector, trying to incentivize and encourage companies to turn some R&D to figuring out how to make cook stoves that would be appealing to consumers and get the cost low enough." [Remarks at London Drug Toronto, 11/4/13]

Chapter 18

EUROPE

Hillary Clinton: "Unless the National Leaders and the European Union and Eurozone Leaders Get Their Act Together, You Will See Some Pretty Unpredictable Leaders and Political Parties Coming to the Forefront."

"So I would certainly not count the Europeans out, but I think they have a lot of work to do. And I'm actually more concerned from another perspective. I think that unless the national leaders and the European Union and Eurozone leaders get their act together, you will see some pretty unpredictable leaders and political parties coming to the forefront in a lot of countries. You'll see a lot of nationalism. You will see a lot of chauvinism. You'll see UK parties that is—winning elections in UK is going to push Cameron and his coalition government to the right as it moves towards an election—I think in 2015. What does that mean for Europe? What does that mean for our relationship?" [Speech to Goldman Sachs, 2013 IBD CEO Annual Conference, 6/4/13]

Chapter 19

GOVERNMENT SURVEILLANCE

Clinton Criticized Snowden for Exposing Sensitive Information to China, Russia, Iran, and Others.

CLINTON: Now as to Snowden, I am of the mind that he did a great service to China, Russia, Iran and others. And he did a wakeup call for the United States to engage in this debate. But it is beyond my comprehension how someone could abscond with so much material that is so sensitive, because it's not just whether or not somebody was listening to Angela Merkel, it is so much deeper and broader, and really does address serious threats and dangers to us, and to either intentionally or unintentionally turn that over to the Chinese and the Russians is really troubling to me. So I'll just lay it on the table. Some people think he's quite a heroic figure. I don't. I don't. I think he could have been whistleblower. If he really cared about raising some of these issues and stayed right here in the United States, there's a lot of whistleblower protections. He did not have to run off to Hong Kong. He did not have to take laptops. When we used to go into Hong Kong, China, or Russia, we left every piece of electronic equipment with the batteries out on our plane. So I think there's more to this story that will eventually over time unspool, but your main point that we need to have a thorough debate to protect Americans privacy I agree with 100 percent. As somebody who has had my privacy scrutinized and violated for decades, I'm all for privacy, believe me. [Clinton Speech for JP Morgan, 4/22/14]

Clinton Described WikiLeaks as Exemplifying the Line between Endangering the Line between Liberty and Privacy, Said State Department and Defense Department Agreed to Share Cables before She Started.

"How do we deal with that without crossing the line and endangering people's liberty and privacy is going to be a very big issue for us. Now, that's somewhat exemplified, but not totally in the same framework, by the WikiLeaks problem. WikiLeaks came about because the military, in their efforts to do counterinsurgency, particularly in Iraq and that region, and also in Afghanistan but not exclusively, wanted to provide their intelligence officers and even commanders with more context and texture, like, you know, if I'm a captain and I'm going off to negotiate with some sheikh in Mosul, I'd better know a little bit more about what he believes and who he is and on and on. So before I got there, the Defense Department asked the State Department if the State Department would share what are called cables, sort of a diplomatic tool that is being overtaken by email and the like, but nevertheless, reporting cables, and the State Department agreed and were told that this was a very secure site. And it might have been secure if you were an Iranian or a Chinese hacker but it wasn't secure from Private Manning who became convinced that he needed to pass this information on to WikiLeaks." [Remarks at Mediacorp, 11/13/13]

Government Surveillance 75

Clinton Said the Lesson from WikiLeaks and Snowden Is That Even Encrypted Information Can Be Hacked and Said She Doesn't Know How to Protect against Employees Who Were Supposedly Vetted.

"Now, what did we learn from that? Well, we learned, as we learned again with Snowden, that we have so much information on the internet, even if you encrypt it, even if you think it's the most secure site in the world that the Chinese will not be able to get into it, even the Russians who are constantly knocking on the door can't get into it, somebody in your own operation can get into it. And in order to guard against that, you would have to have so many more layers of bureaucracy and encryption that was available through jumping through hoops and the like that you don't really know how to protect against the very people that you have vetted, supposedly, and employed." [Remarks at Mediacorp, 11/13/13]

Clinton Said Criticism of Government Surveillance Was in Part Because Information about the Program Leaked That Was "Not in Context and It's Not Clearly Explainable or Understood."

"So trying to go up to the line of what is appropriate surveillance and security measures and not over the line is something we need to have a full comprehensive discussion about. Because what we need to do to keep ourselves and our friends secure, people need to know about it. Maybe not in all the details, because we also don't want to alert adversaries, but in enough detail so people can say, Okay, they're not really listening to my conversation when I, you know, call home and talk to my daughter, whatever. And I think part of the problem has arisen because the stuff that has been leaked is sort of bits and pieces. It's not in context and it's not clearly explainable or understood." [Speech at Colgate University, 10/25/13]

Hillary Clinton "Fully" Supported What President Obama and Congress Were Trying to Do on Privacy.

"I start from the vantage point that this is a constant tension, and because we are now so much more advanced in what we can learn about people, not just in governments, private sector holds far more information about individuals than the government does, it's just the way that business is done today, then we have to keep striking the right balance. And I think what the president has begun to do and what the Congress is trying to do is something that I fully support." [Hillary Clinton Remarks at Nexenta, 8/28/14]

Hillary Clinton: NSA Didn't "Cross Legal Lines" but Sat on Them.

"I think it's fair to say that the government, the NSA didn't so far as we know cross legal lines but they came right up and sat on them. And when people understood that it could perhaps mean that their data was being collected in these gigantic metadata configurations, that that was somehow threatening." [Hillary Clinton Remarks at Nexenta, 8/28/14]

Hillary Clinton Noted the "Huge Brouhaha over Surveillance and the Fights That Are Incumbent upon the United States and Our Intelligence Services to Respond To."

"So on the headlines, if you look around right now, obviously people are focused on the Middle East, which is a perennial crisis. In Syria, what's happening with the charm offensive by Iran and the negotiations that are taking place on the nuclear program. The somewhat slow but I think glib signs of some economic activity finally in parts of Europe, but that's combined with the huge brouhaha over surveillance and the fights that are incumbent upon the United States and our intelligence services to respond to." [Goldman Sachs Builders and Innovators Summit, 10/29/13]

Government Surveillance

77

Hillary Clinton Said Bin Laden Was Found by Intercepting a Phone Call, Not from a Walk in Tip.

"I was in the small group that recommended to the President that he go after bin Laden. The amount of work that was required to get a strong enough basis of information on which to plan took more than a decade. The people who were the analysts and collectors and good old-fashioned spies who were gathering bits and pieces of information, some of them from cell phone conversations, I will tell you, and then all of a sudden putting this matrix together and saying this guy used to protect bin Laden. He has just made a phone call. He said this in the phone call. We need to figure out where he is. Then we need to follow him and that is how we found this compound in Abbottabad. It didn't happen because somebody walked into our embassy and said, You know, there is a suspicious compound in Abbottabad that you guys should go take a look at." [Remarks at London Drug Toronto, 11/4/13]

Hillary Clinton Talked about Her Apology Tour after WikiLeaks and Said Some Leaders Actually Cried, with the Implication It Was Silvio Berlusconi.

"SECRETARY CLINTON: Okay. I was Secretary of State when WikiLeaks happened. You remember that whole debacle.

So out come hundreds of thousands of documents. And I have to go on an apology tour. And I had a jacket made like a rock star tour. The Clinton Apology Tour. I had to go and apologize to anybody who was in any way characterized in any of the cables in any way that might be considered less than flattering. And it was painful. Leaders who shall remain nameless, who were characterized as vain, egotistical, power hungry—MR. BLANKFEIN: Proved it. SECRETARY CLINTON: — corrupt. And we knew they were. This was not fiction. And I had to go and say, you know, our ambassadors, they get carried away, they want to all be literary people. They go off on tangents. What can I say? I had grown men cry. I mean, literally. I am a friend of America, and you say these things about me. MR. BLANKFEIN: That's an Italian accent. SECRETARY CLINTON: Have a sense of humor." Goldman Sachs Builders and Innovators Summit, 10/29/13]

Hillary Clinton: "There's No Doubt That Much of What We've Done since 9/11 Has Kept Us Safer. That's Just a Fact. It's Also Kept Our Friends and Our Partners and Our Allies Safer, as Well."

"SECRETARY CLINTON: So, fast forward. Here we are. You know, look, I have said, and I will continue to say, we do need to have a conversation with and take a hard look at the right balance that we could strike between, you know, privacy and security because there's no doubt, and I've seen this and understand it, there's no doubt that much of what we've done since 9/11 has kept us safer. That's just a fact. It's also kept our friends and our partners and our allies safer, as well. The sharing of intelligence requires the gathering of intelligence and the analysis of intelligence." [Goldman Sachs Builders and Innovators Summit, 10/29/13]

Hillary Clinton: "But the Collection of the Metadata Is Something That Has Proven to Be Very Useful."

"SECRETARY CLINTON: Well, we do better. I mean, that's the problem. We have a lot of information. And not the kind of information that most of our citizens are worried about because I really have no evidence and have no reason to believe that, you know, we've got people listening to American citizens' conversations. But the collection of the metadata is something that has proven to be very useful." [Goldman Sachs Builders and Innovators Summit, 10/29/13]

Hillary Clinton Said We Needed to Reassure Citizens and Allies Nothing Is Being Collected beyond What Is Necessary.

"So I think maybe we should be honest that, you know, maybe we've gone too far, but then let's have a conversation about what too far means and how we protect privacy to give our own citizens the

Government Surveillance

79

reassurance that they are not being spied by their own government, give our friends and allies the reassurance that we're not going beyond what is the necessary collection and analysis that we share with them and try to have a mature conversation." [Goldman Sachs Builders and Innovators Summit, 10/29/13]

Hillary Clinton Said WikiLeaks Resulted in Vulnerable Individuals Being Moved after Being Exposed.

"SECRETARY CLINTON: Well, separate the two. The WikiLeaks problem put at risk certain individuals. We had to—we had to form a kind of investigative team that looked at all the names and all the documents, which was quite a challenge, to make sure that identities that were either revealed or described in enough detail that they could be determined would not put people who were at risk. I mean, without going into detail, you know, maybe they're—let's just hypothetically say there was somebody serving in a military in a certain country who was worried about some of the activities of the military that he served because he thought they were doing business with rogue states or terrorist networks, and so he would seek out an American diplomat to begin a conversation. And the American diplomat would report back about the concerns that were being expressed about what was happening in this country. And then it's—you know, it's exposed to the world. So we had to identify, and we moved a number of people to safe—to safety out of where they were in order for them to be not vulnerable." [Goldman Sachs Builders and Innovators Summit, 10/29/13]

Hillary: "Private Manning Should Have Never Had Access to a Lot of What He Did Have Access To. So, in Effect, It Was a Problem."

"So on the WikiLeaks, there was the embarrassment factor, there were the potential vulnerability factors that individuals faced. The WikiLeaks issue was, you know, unfortunate. Private Manning should have never had access to a lot of what he did have access to. So, in effect, it was a problem. But it didn't expose the guts of how we collect and analyze data" [Goldman Sachs Builders and Innovators Summit, 10/29/13]

Hillary Clinton Said the Snowden Leak Was a "Real Loss of Important Information" and Noted Iranian Cyber Attacks Were Getting Worse.

"So I do think that there has been a real loss of important information that shouldn't belong to or be made available to people who spend a lot of their time trying to penetrate our government, our businesses. And even worse, you know, some who are engaged in terrorist activities. I mean, the Iranians did a disruption of service attack on American banks a year ago. The Iranians are getting much more sophisticated. They run the largest terrorist networks in the world." [Goldman Sachs Builders and Innovators Summit, 10/29/13]

Hillary Clinton: "So I Think That WikiLeaks Was a Big Bump in the Road, but I Think the Snowden Material Could Be Potentially Much More Threatening to Us."

"So, you know, if Snowden has given them a blueprint to how we operate, why is that in any way a positive. We should have the debate. We should have the conversation. We should make the changes where they're necessary. But we shouldn't put our systems and our people at risk. So I think that WikiLeaks was a big bump in the road, but I think the Snowden material could be potentially much more threatening to us." [Goldman Sachs Builders and Innovators Summit, 10/29/13]

Chapter 20

GUNS

Hillary Clinton Opposed Blind People Having Right to Guns.
"Well, I very much supported what my husband did when he was President, which was to ban assault weapons and large magazines. And it was a very contentious debate. Some of you may have followed it. But, it was part of a broader anti-crime initiative, including police on the streets and much more effort into community policing and the like. And I thought that it was a necessarily part of that. It was a law that is what we call in Washington it sunsetted. So it went out at the end of 10 years. And since then there has been a concerted effort by the gun lobby to basically end all restrictions on guns. And I don't think that's what is called for under the Constitution. I think that there are a number of sensible steps that can and should be taken. [...] And one of the new claims that they're making is that blind people deserve to have their Constitutional rights, and deserve to have guns. And that you kind of think to yourself, that's almost beyond imagination. And it's pushing and pushing and pushing because there's no push back." [Hillary Clinton Remarks at Nexenta, 8/28/14]

Chapter 21

HAITI

Clinton: "Brazil Has Led a Police Mission in Haiti for Years That Has Been Dramatically Successful."

"I think that there are some very difficult cases that call into question outcomes. But there are a lot of others, other quieter cases where there have been UN organized and directed interventions that have really saved lives and helped people. You know, Brazil has led a police mission in Haiti for years that has been dramatically successful, and there are many other examples that I could point to." [Clinton Remarks at Boston Consulting Group, 6/20/13]

Hillary Clinton Noted That She Sat down with All the Presidential Candidates in Haiti and Democracy Survived When Michel Martelly Became President.

"But it was very complicated inside Haiti because the now president President Martelly, emerged as the top vote getter and there were a lot of people who said we're not going to go along with this, we can't accept the fact that a majority of people who voted in the election voted for him. So I sit down to meet with all of the candidates plus President Preval because I thought it was important to help them talk through what they were facing because it would have setback the recovery of Haiti, it would have dried up donors money, if the results of an election denied the people their vote and yet at the same time it wouldn't be helpful, I didn't think, to, you know, stage press conferences and, you know, wave my arms and, you know, talk about the sanctity of the vote and condemn anybody who was trying to undermine it. I wanted to find a path to the right thing that would not embarrass anyone involved and give people a chance to save face. So we talked a lot about what it means to be a leader, with all the parties that were going to influence the final decision and in particular with President Preval who had given so much to his country and had suffered so much because of the earthquake, which leveled the Presidential Palace and killed so many people whom he knew and cared about. This was his defining moment. He was either going to be remembered as another in a long line of Haitian leaders who did not respect democracy or as the president, who, despite the worst possible circumstances, protected democracy. He had to choose. I think it was helpful that I was a former politician so I could sit there knee to knee and say, you know, I've won elections and I've lost elections, there's life after both. Democracy is not for the faint hearted. And I said, you got to do the hard thing because ultimately that will serve your country and your reputation. He agreed. Democracy - survived. Martelly became president." [05162013 Remarks to Banco Itau.doc, p. 24-25]

Chapter 22

HEALTH CARE

AFFORDABLE CARE ACT

Hillary Clinton Said She Wants Us to Have a Debate Where Our Differences Are Fully Aired on Healthcare Reform since There Are Different Approaches.

"Now, what does that have to do with health care reform? Well, I want to see us have a debate where our differences are fully aired because, clearly, there are different approaches about what we think can work. We don't have one size fit all. Our country is quite diverse. What works in New York City is not necessarily going to work in Harrison, Arkansas or Albuquerque, so we do need to have people who are looking for common ways of approaching problems using evidence but leaving their blaming, their gaming, their shaming, point scoring at the door. Because when we think about it, our country is such a remarkable accomplishment. Think about how diverse we are. We've had lots of disagreements. We even had a civil war for heaven sakes, so it's not like we just—you know, like in those drug commercials where we just hold hands and dance through the meadows while somebody is telling you everything that can go wrong like your ear's falling off if you take the drug they're advertising." [02262014 HWA Remarks at HIMMS [Orlando].DOC, p. 10]

Clinton Said American People Were "Right" to Be Frustrated by Slow ACA Website but to Remember Historical Context of Slow Starts for Medicare Part D and Massachusetts Health Care.

"So President Obama and the American people are right to be frustrated by the technical problems with HealthCare.gov, the new health care website -- too slow, too many people getting stuck instead of getting served, and as the President has said, there is no excuse for this. But I think it's important to put it into some historical context. It was the same when President Bush rolled out Medicare Part D in 2005. I was a senator serving the people of New York. And our seniors were even less prepared to navigate the difficulties of understanding what they wanted and then figuring out how to sign up for it. It was the same in Massachusetts when the health care plan signed into law by then Governor Romney came into effect. It was plagued by early glitches, and only about 100 people signed up the first month." [Remarks at Beaumont Society Dinner, 11/6/13]

Clinton Said People Should Have Been Told to Expect Problems with ACA Website Ahead of Time.

"So I knew there would always be trouble, and I think everybody who thought about it, there would be. So I would make these—these three quick points: First, I think more people should have been told that so that we didn't have this idea that on October 1, you just turn on your computer and it's, like, magically going to respond to every one of your questions. I assume that it's going to get fixed, the sooner the better, because there is a lot of good information and comparison shopping

Health Care 87

that's never been available in the health insurance market before."
[Remarks to New York Tri-State of the Market, 11/14/13]

Clinton Said President Obama Spent More Time Than Democrats Wanted Him to Trying to Get Some Republicans to Support Health Care Reform.

"So you can get to the point of saying, okay, we can live with this, you say you can live with that, I can sell it to the Democrats, you sell it to the Republicans, and the answer would come back, I can't sell it to Republicans, so we have to jigger it around somehow. Whether that was a negotiating tactic or the hard reality that it was hard to sell it to the caucus, I don't know. But I do remember quite well the President working diligently to reach out to people and trying very hard on the health care bill, for example, spending more time than a lot of Democrats wanted him to, trying to figure out how he can get some Republicans on board." [Goldman Sachs AIMS Alternative Investments Symposium, 10/24/13]

Clinton Said She Was "Sure That We'll Be Struggling" with ACA Implementation "for Some Time to Come."

"MODERATOR KRUEGER: One last easy, quick question: Health care. SECRETARY CLINTON: He's known for his sense of humor. MODERATOR KRUEGER: We now spend 18 percent, going up to 20 percent of our United States economy, the largest economy in the world, on health care. Recent articles seem to be that ObamaCare, the Affordable Healthcare Act, is going to increase that over time. What country is doing it best out there? The next developed industrialized country spends about ten-and-a-half percent of their economy on health care. What country is doing its best, or if we started with a blank canvas, what would we do? SECRETARY CLINTON: Well, first I have to say that I think the jury is out, because the implementation of the Affordable Care Act is going on as we speak. There are some very important features in that, you know, publicizing costs of medical procedures, which is giving a lot of food for thought about why does the same procedure cost three times as much three hundred miles away from where it's done somewhere else; looking at how we try to tie prevention to outcomes more effectively. I mean, I think there are a lot of very good parts of it. Now, implementing something this big is complicated, and I'm sure that we'll be struggling with it for some time to come, but I think there are important measures that are included." [Hillary Clinton remarks to ECGR Grand Rapids, 6/17/13]

EMPLOYER-BASED MODEL

Clinton Said the US Seems "to Be Wedded to" Employer-Based Health Insurance, "It Would Be Very Difficult to Get a Consensus Politically" to Change That.

"So we have made a decision built on an old World War II program that was using health benefits as a way of keeping people in the workforce and being competitive, linked to employment. That is very costly, and we also moved over time from what used to be non-profit insurance companies to mostly for-profit insurance companies today. People are entitled to make a profit, but that drives up costs, and we we you know we have that built into this 18, 20 percent GDP. So we made decisions and we seem to be wedded to those decisions. So it would be very difficult to get a consensus politically that would dramatically change. I mean, if you look at the Affordable Care Act, it starts with an employer-based system. Most people who have in the private sector insurance won't see much change, depending upon, you know, what the pricing structure does. But their basic policies will remain as they are." [Hillary Clinton remarks to ECGR Grand Rapids, 6/17/13]

Health Care

IMPROVING ON THE FEE-FOR-SERVICE MODEL

Clinton: "Ultimately How Might We Replace Our Fee for Service Model with Provider Led Community-Wide Care That Can Compete on Quality and Reward Value over Volume?"
[1/27/14, HWA Remarks at Premier Health]

Clinton: "At Some Point We Have to Move Away from Fee-for-Service Payments for Medical Care."
"I also in my statement alluded to the idea that at some point we have to move away from fee for service payments for medical care. It is not serving physicians well or any other health care provider, and I don't believe it's serving patients well." [4/11/14, Remarks at California Medical Association]

Clinton: "How Might We Begin to Replace the Fee-for-Service Model with Provider-Led, Community-Wide Care That Can Compete on Quality and Reward Value over Volume?"
"How might we begin to replace the fee-for-service model with provider-led, community-wide care that can compete on quality and reward value over volume? And while we try to maintain what makes the American health care system so special and extraordinarily effective, how do we work more closely with our research and scientific community, with our engineers, with our businesses so that new ideas get to market faster, can influence care and be taken to the next level?" [Remarks to Cardiovascular Research Foundation, 9/15/14]

Clinton: "...The Fee-for-Service Model, Which Made a Lot of Sense for a Long Time, May Not Make Sense."
"But most of what I see that has to be done in the future in my view should be led by a partnership of purpose between physicians and other caregivers and patients and payers. And the fact is that a lot of the cost in our system, which is not related to paying physicians,

paying for research, paying for prevention, and all the things that we think would lead to better outcomes. We have to make a very principled decision, do we want to continue paying for that or is there a better way to pay? And that's why I said in my remarks the fee-for-service model, which made a lot of sense for a long time, may not make sense. It may not make sense for physicians or hospitals or any other provider, and it may not make sense for patients and payers. And I think we need to have as evidence-based, as mature a conversation as we can manage in our society at large." [Remarks to Cardiovascular Research Foundation, 9/15/14]

LOWERING COSTS

Hillary Clinton: "Businesses Pay Taxes" on Health Care Even in Single-Payer Systems, "so Businesses Also Have a Direct Interest in Getting the Cost of Health Care to Be Lower."

"So employers in the United States have a very direct stake in trying to assure that their employees and their employees' families are healthier, because they end up bearing part of the cost burden when that is not the case. We just had a very widely reported incident of an executive of a major American company, you know, complaining that two babies born with serious health problems had each cost the company a million dollars. Well, there has to be a recognition that maybe some kinds of health problems cannot be avoided. They're genetic, they're congenital, they're accidental, they're infectious, but some kinds of health problems, particularly what we're talking about, the chronic disease load can be mitigated against. And so businesses have that direct opportunity, but even in other countries where you don't have an employer-based system but a single-payer system, businesses pay taxes. So businesses also have a direct interest in getting

Health Care

91

the cost of health care to be lower." [Hillary Clinton Remarks for the Novo Nordisk Diabetes Conference, 2/14/14]

MEDICAL DEVICES

Hillary Clinton Said She Worked Closely with the Medical Device Industry as Senator and Understands the "Critical Role" the Industry Plays.

HILLARY CLINTON: "The Affordable Care Act also promotes innovation and incentivizes solutions that emphasize the quality of medical care, not just the quantity, and medical technology is at the heart of this effort. Many of the innovations that will allow us both to provide care that is medically sound and cost-effective will come from companies represented in this room. When I was a Senator from New York, I worked with the medical device industry on a number of important issues, and I understand how critical the role that you play is. And yes, I know that you have important questions that you would like addressed. But my view is that we need to keep working toward win-win solutions, improving what we have in sensible ways that will lead to lower costs, greater insurance at affordable costs for everyone, higher transparency for consumers who, after all, bear more and more of the burdens of out of pocket costs." [Remarks for AdvaMed, 10/8/14]

Rx

Clinton Disputed a Claim That She Proposed Price Controls on Drugs in the 90s, Arguing That She Proposed Greater Competition, Which Is More Effective in Managing Costs.

MR. SVOKOS: "Secretary Clinton, this is a room filled with individuals from the pharmaceutical industry. The policies that you proposed to contain health care costs in the '90s, mainly price controls, were not exactly popular with our industry at the time. Has your opinion changed since then? What policies would you propose today? SECRETARY CLINTON: Well, I have to start by saying I don't think we proposed price controls. We proposed more competition, more transparency, state exchanges, if those sound familiar, to entice greater negotiation over price. And I still believe in greater negotiation over price." [Hillary Clinton Remarks at DCAT – New York City, 3/13/14]

SINGLE-PAYER HEALTH CARE

Clinton Said Single-Payer Health Care Systems "Can Get Costs Down," and "Is as Good or Better on Primary Care," but "They Do Impose Things like Waiting Times."

"If you look at countries that are comparable, like Switzerland or Germany, for example, they have mixed systems. They don't have just a single-payer system, but they have very clear controls over budgeting and accountability. If you look at the single-payer systems, like Scandinavia, Canada, and elsewhere, they can get costs down because, you know, although their care, according to statistics, overall is as good or better on primary care, in particular, they do impose things like waiting times, you know. It takes longer to get like a hip replacement than it might take here." [Hillary Clinton remarks to ECGR Grand Rapids, 6/17/13]

UNIVERSAL COVERAGE

Clinton Said Her Goal in the 90s Was to Create a Universal Health Care System around the Employer-Based System, Which the Affordable Care Act Achieved.

"And so we were trying to build a universal system around the employer-based system. And indeed now with President Obama's

Health Care 93

legislative success in getting the Affordable Care Act passed that is what we've done. We still have primarily an employer-based system, but we now have people able to get subsidized insurance. So we have health insurance companies playing a major role in the provision of healthcare, both to the employed whose employers provide health insurance, and to those who are working but on their own are not able to afford it and their employers either don't provide it, or don't provide it at an affordable price." [Hillary Clinton Remarks for tinePublic – Saskatoon, Canada, 1/21/14]

Clinton Cited President Johnson's Success in Establishing Medicare and Medicaid and Said She Wanted to See the US Have Universal Health Care like in Canada.

"You know, on healthcare we are the prisoner of our past. The way we got to develop any kind of medical insurance program was during World War II when companies facing shortages of workers began to offer healthcare benefits as an inducement for employment. So from the early 1940s healthcare was seen as a privilege connected to employment. And after the war when soldiers came back and went back into the market there was a lot of competition, because the economy was so heated up. So that model continued. And then of course our large labor unions bargained for healthcare with the employers that their members worked for. So from the early 1940s until the early 1960s we did not have any Medicare, or our program for the poor called Medicaid until President Johnson was able to get both passed in 1965. So the employer model continued as the primary means by which working people got health insurance. People over 65 were eligible for Medicare. Medicaid, which was a partnership, a funding partnership between the federal government and state governments, provided some, but by no means all poor people with access to healthcare. So what we've been struggling with certainly Harry Truman, then Johnson was successful on Medicare and Medicaid, but didn't touch the employer based system, then actually Richard Nixon made a proposal that didn't go anywhere, but was quite far reaching. Then with my husband's administration we worked very hard to come up with a system, but we were very much constricted by the political realities that if you had your insurance from your employer you were reluctant to try anything else. And so we were trying to build a universal system around the employer-based system. And indeed now with President Obama's legislative success in getting the Affordable Care Act passed that is what we've done. We still have primarily an employer-based system, but we now have people able to get subsidized insurance. So we have health insurance companies playing a major role in the provision of healthcare, both to the employed whose employers provide health insurance, and to those who are working but on their own are not able to afford it and their employers either don't provide it, or don't provide it at an affordable price. We are still struggling. We've made a lot of progress. Ten million Americans now have insurance who didn't have it before the Affordable Care Act, and that is a great step forward. (Applause.) And what we're going to have to continue to do is monitor what the costs are and watch closely to see whether employers drop more people from insurance so that they go into what we call the health exchange system. So we're really just at the beginning. But we do have Medicare for people over 65. And you couldn't, I don't think, take it away if you tried, because people are very satisfied with it, but we also have a lot of political and financial resistance to expanding that system to more people. So we're in a learning period as we move forward with the implementation of the Affordable Care Act. And I'm hoping that whatever the shortfalls or the glitches have been, which in a big piece of legislation you're going to have, those will be remedied and we can really take a hard look at what's succeeding, fix what isn't, and keep moving forward to get to affordable universal healthcare coverage like you have here in Canada. [Clinton Speech For tinePublic – Saskatoon, CA, 1/21/15]

Health Care 95

CANADA

Hillary Clinton Praised London Drugs' Role in the Canadian Health System.

"So London Drugs is ahead of the curve in ways big and small. Employees are now equipped with iPads to help customers access product reviews, explore product specifications. More information in the hands of consumers is becoming and I think will increasingly become a huge competitive advantage. Each new store comes with what is called a Learning Lab with public seminars about key issues like preventive health, and that is really important not only in Canada but in our country and elsewhere because drugstores often represent the most accessible point of access to the entire health care system. So in many ways, what I have learned about London Drugs is that they are really trying to be creative and co-operative, I just saw the partnerships that were highlighted, moving more toward wellness, toward prevention, toward community-based, lower-cost, better results-driven health care." [Remarks at London Drug Toronto, 11/4/13]

Hillary Clinton Praised London Drugs for Provider Customers with Direct Access to Health Care Services

"And it is good news that a lot of drugstore and retail chains, and certainly London Drugs has been a leader in this, are helping their customers get access to direct health care services. You can get a flu shot. You can consult with a nurse practitioner. You can address minor and even chronic illnesses that would cost much more to treat in traditional medical settings." [Remarks at London Drug Toronto, 11/4/13]

Chapter 23

HELPING CORPORATIONS

Hillary Clinton Noted That as a Senator Executives from Corning Glass Saw Her about China Preventing Them from Entering New Markets There.

"First, let's go back to 2004. I was representing New York in the Senate, and a group of executives from Corning Glass, a great New York company, came to see me. It's famous for supplying the scratch resistant Gorilla Glass, used by many smart phones and tablets, including the iPhone. And Corning spends more than $700 million a year on research. And beyond glass, they produce advanced liquid crystal displays in computer monitors and televisions, as well as optical fiber and cable for the communications industry, clean filters for diesel engines, a wide range of other innovative products that they have invested in creating. Their technology and products were so good that competitors in China felt they needed an unfair advantage to compete against Corning. So they went to the Chinese government, asking it either to block Corning from entering new markets altogether or slap their fiber optics with absurdly high tariffs, which would be the same result, they could not compete any longer. And there were blatant attempts to steal the company's intellectual property, some of which

98   *Christian Mellor*

unfortunately succeeded. Now, this was blatantly unfair and also a threat to the future of a company that employed thousands of Americans." [06262014 HWA Remarks for GTCR (Chicago, IL).docx, p. 2]

Hillary Clinton Said She Raised the Corning Matter to President Bush When He Came to the Opening of Bill Clinton's Library in Little Rock in 2004.

"So, hearing about the situation, I invited the Chinese ambassador to my Senate office, sent a pointed letter to the Chinese minister of trade, made every attempt I could to enlist the Bush administration to back me up. But that turned out to be harder than it sounds because of a philosophical difference about what our government should do, if anything, to support American businesses competing and operating in foreign markets. We're having that debate again over the Export Import Bank. You know, it's ideological. There are a lot of members of Congress who say, the U.S. government should not try to help an American business be competitive in a foreign market, the way our competitors help their businesses. Let the markets work. Well, now, that's great and we know that would be ideal, but that's not the world in which we live today. In this case it would mean leaving an American company at the mercy of unfair competition, on a playing field that was anything but level. So after striking out with members of the administration, I raised the Corning matter directly with President Bush in 2004 when he came to Little Rock for the opening of my husband's presidential library." [06262014 HWA Remarks for GTCR (Chicago, IL).docx, p. 2-3]

Hillary Clinton Said after President Bush Intervened, China Dropped the Discriminatory Tariffs and Corning's Business Thrived.

"And I told him, this is a great American company, it's being threatened, and, Mr. President, your administration needs to help me help them. And to his credit, President Bush agreed to look into the

Helping Corporations 99

problem and he did. And that December, China dropped the discriminatory tariffs. And when it was allowed to compete on a level playing field, Corning's business thrived." [06262014 HWA Remarks for GTCR (Chicago, IL).docx, p. 3]

Hillary Clinton Said as Secretary of State, She Helped Open New Markets and Boosted Exports.

"And so when I left the Senate, became Secretary of State, I focused on two big questions: Could we sustain and create good jobs at home, and help speed our recovery by opening new markets and boosting exports, and were we going to let China and other relatively closed markets in which state-owned enterprises dominated rewrite the rules of the global economy in a way that would disadvantage American workers and companies." [06262014 HWA Remarks for GTCR (Chicago, IL).docx, p. 4]

Hillary Clinton Said She Went to Bat for FedEx When China Wouldn't Issue Them Licenses for Delivery Companies to Operate.

"And this is true for long-established businesses. I got a call one day in the State Department from Fred Smith, the founder and still driving force behind FedEx. FedEx had been in China for years, and it was in hundreds of markets in China. Where there was an airport they could land their planes, FedEx was operating. And all of a sudden, the state had said to FedEx, "Sorry, we're changing the way we give licenses for delivery companies to operate. So you will have to apply for new licenses for your more than 400 sites, no guarantee you will get any." By the time Fred called me, they had about eight, with no potential that they could count on that they would get the remaining licenses. And again I went to bat for them, had our ambassador also intervene, and began to push as hard as we could. And the only reason we made any progress is because America's standing, working with the United States as part of a strategic relationship, was important enough to the Chinese to give the orders to open the doors to make sure FedEx still had enough licenses to operate." [06262014 HWA Remarks for GTCR (Chicago, IL).docx, p. 4]

Hillary Clinton Discussed Her Work Helping Corning Deal with Chinese Trade Barriers.

"I'll give you a quick example from my senate years. Corning is a great upstate company in Corning, New York, and they sell very sophisticated glass products and they've spent a lot of money, you know, researching and developing those products in fiberoptics and all the rest, and they've done business in China for a long time. And, you know, as China develops their own indigenous industries, they often put increasing barriers in front of other companies, most certainly American. So Corning came to me and said, you know, we—we've got a real problem because they're putting these tariffs on us. And this is was during the Bush Administration. [...] So I personally raised this with President Bush, and I said, you know, I'm trying to help a New York company fight against unfair burdens with these tariffs and I need help from the administration. And to his credit, he said, you know, I'll find out what we can do. And we worked together and solved that problem. Fast forward: So I'm in the State Department. And, you know, about five, six years have passed and now, once again, they're facing real, real burdens from the Chinese government. And once again, now I'm Secretary of State. We raise it, we keep raising it." [Hamilton College Speech, 10/4/13]

Clinton Praised Bob Hormats for His Role in Spurring Economic Development from Private Corporations to Either Supplement or "Replace Government Dollars Eventually."

HILLARY CLINTON: Now, JPMorgan is not in the agricultural business, but you have clients and customers around the world who are. Creating sustainable markets that can begin to address the different needs that you would find in dry land farming compared to rainy season farming, and then how we get seeds and fertilizer and

Helping Corporations

101

other inputs, that ultimately has to be a private sector initiative. But the private sector is not going to go in there on its own, because they don't know who they're supposed to talk to. Sometimes you have to open doors of governments to get them in the door. And so working with private sector partners like JPMorgan and trying to find ways to leverage those private dollars enables us to do more in the public sector and then see it transform into the business sector that then gives more opportunities for businesses in those areas and gives better support to farmers. PETER SCHER: It's a great partnership. It's a great example—HILLARY CLINTON: Yeah, and Bob Hormats is sitting there. He was—PETER SCHER: I know he is. HILLARY CLINTON: He was an instrumental partner in a lot of what we did in the economic area to try to begin to think differently about how to use dollars that weren't government dollars, either to supplement government dollars or to replace government dollars eventually. And that's what we aimed at. PETER SCHER: It's a great to leverage for your dollars. [Clinton Speech for JP Morgan, 4/22/14]

Clinton Regaled a Story of How She Fought for Private Express Delivery Service Companies' Access to Chinese Market as Secretary of State.

"Now, let me share a story that Secretary John Bryson knows well. For many years both FedEx and UPS have done profitable business in China. By 2009, FedEx was operating in nearly 60 locations across China, and UPS in 30. But then China imposed new postal laws that required domestic operating permits for express delivery service companies. And the move was widely seen, I think correctly, as a way for Beijing to put its thumb on the scales for the state-controlled China Post. Both FedEx and UPS rightly worried they would receive severely restrictive licenses that would curtail where and how they could do business. And they kept doing their best to make the argument in Beijing to anybody they could buttonhole, but they weren't making much progress. They were finding it very difficult to fight city hall, or in this case fight the Chinese government. So Fred Smith picked up the phone, somebody I've known since Arkansas days, and called me at the State Department to explain the dilemma and ask for help. It was one of many times that American businesses came looking for assistance in competing on a level playing field, and, in fact, where they were competing was anything but level. So our diplomats in Beijing raised the issue at the highest levels of the Chinese government but to no avail. I brought the matter up directly with then Vice Premier Wang Qishan. Secretary Bryson and I followed up with a joint letter, and we kept the pressure on. We made it clear that the U.S. government was not going to sit on the sidelines in the face of unfair competition to two of our important companies. That caught the Chinese by surprise, as they later admitted, because they were used to a much more laissez faire attitude. Well, that was then and this is now. The new tone began to get results, and eventually the Chinese pledged that over the course of a three-year period they would grant more permits. And although the issue is far from settled, both FedEx and UPS are still operating in China and have a base that they still expect to be able to expand from." [Clinton Remarks to Deutsche Bank, 10/7/14]

Jeff Immelt Cited His Relationship with Bob Hormats as a Positive from Clinton's Time at State.

"The State Department I would say and the aspect of selling completely changed when Secretary Clinton came in office. For those of us that have been leveraging or trying to get involved with selling our goods around the world, I think it was the sense of okay, do the best you can, and then we're right behind you if you get in trouble. The government will be there at some point. And when Secretary Clinton and a guy named Bob Hormats who was a Goldman Sachs guy that we all knew for a long time, it all changed where we were on offense all the time. State was in the lead frequently when we were trying to do

Helping Corporations 103

that, and I think it helped the business context for the company massively, and that's really what I think the Secretary did on our behalf, so fantastic." [Clinton Speech for General Electric's Global Leadership Meeting – Boca Raton, FL, 1/6/14]

Clinton Thanked Jeff Immelt for His Advice on Exports and Said Bob Hormats Was Her Partner.

"You know, let me say that, first of all, I want to thank you personally for sharing the counsel on exports because I thought we needed to be more competitive and more on the offense after '08. So when I came in that was a major effort of mine, which we call economic skin graft, and Bob Hormats was my partner, and we worked very hard to do two things: One to try to clear the way of companies that were competing and out there trying to do the right thing like GE, but, secondly, trying to get more companies to go compete." [Clinton Speech for General Electric's Global Leadership Meeting—Boca Raton, FL, 1/6/14]

Hillary Clinton: "I Visited the Boeing Design Center in Moscow... I Made the Case That Boeing's Jet Set the Global Gold Standard."

"In 2010, President Obama set a target of doubling America's exports over five years, and at the State Department I made export promotions a personal mission. So as I traveled the world on behalf of our country, I did everything I could to go to bat for American companies trying to break into new markets and compete on a level playing field. It took me to some really interesting places, particularly now with all the problems we're seeing with Russia and President Putin. Back in 2009, when Dmitri Medvedev was actually president, I visited the Boeing Design Center in Moscow, because Boeing had been trying to secure a contract for new planes with the Russians. And I made the case that Boeing's jet set the global gold standard. And after I left, our embassy kept at it, and in 2010 Russians agreed to buy 50 737s for almost \$4 billion, which translates into thousands of American jobs." [Hillary Clinton Remarks at the Institute of Scrap Recycling Industries Convention, 4/10/14]

Chapter 24

HOUSING

Clinton Said This of the Debate around How to Avoid Another Housing Crisis: "I Really Don't Want to See Decisions Made That Restrict the Opportunities for People to Own Either Commercial or Residential Real Estate."

"So now there's all these policy debates about what to do to avoid ever having happen what did happen back in '07, '08, which I think is absolutely fair and necessary, but I really don't want to see decisions made that constrict the opportunities for people to own either commercial or residential real estate." [Remarks to New York Tri-State of the Market, 11/14/13]

Clinton Said There Are Changes That Need to Be Made to Protect Buyers and Sellers in Real Estate but "It's Very Important We Keep Our Head on Straight."

"I think it's very important that we keep our head on straight. That, yes, if there are changes that have to be made to protect the market, to protect buyers and sellers, to avoid the kind of sequence of events that we all live through, absolutely. But we need to get back to the kind of fulfillment of people's ambitions to own real estate that has been a hallmark of this country." [Remarks to New York Tri-State of the Market, 11/14/13]

Clinton Said She Worked Closely with the National Association of Realtors in the Senate to "Keep the Big Banks out of Real Estate."

"And in talking with the National Association of Realtors last week in San Francisco, it was one of their highest priorities. When I was senator, I worked closely with the National Association on a piece of legislation to keep the big banks out of real estate, because if you remember back in, like, '02, '03, '04, there was this big move for banks to have total vertical integration that they would own the real estate companies, they would run the brokerage outfits, they would take it from, you know, beginning to end. I thought that was a terrible idea then. I think it's a terrible idea now." [Remarks to New York Tri-State of the Market, 11/14/13]

Clinton Said on Real Estate Reforms She Is "in the Camp That Says Do No Harm."

"If we do Fannie and Freddie reforms, you still have to have some kind of backstop for mortgages. So I'm just in the camp that says do no harm. You know, let's figure out how we avoid the mistakes that we all suffered from, but let's not, you know, undermine the ability of people to buy and sell real estate." [Remarks to New York Tri-State of the Market, 11/14/13]

Hillary Clinton Said She Was Proud of Her Work with Realtors "to Advance Legislation to Keep the Big Banks from Moving into Real Estate Brokerages."

"I still have fond memories from the last visit that I made to the National Association of REALTORS back in 2006. And all work we did together during my time representing New York in the Senate. We worked together to advance legislation to keep the big banks from moving into real estate brokerages (applause) (inaudible) -- which have

Housing 107

made the financial crisis even more devastating. We also worked together to expand the federal housing shortage and to look for ways to help families facing foreclosure with concrete steps. You have been good partners, not only to me, but I think to the American people. "[2013 National Association of Realtors Conference and Expo, 11/9/13]

Hillary Clinton: "I Just Tell You What I Believe, and It's Not a Comment on Anybody's Legislation or Lack Thereof, But, I Think We're Still Living in Too Uncertain a World to Make Radical Changes Right Now"

"I just tell you what I believe, and it's not a comment on anybody's legislation or lack thereof, but, I think we're still living in too uncertain a world to make radical changes right now. (Applause) I think there are too many people who still don't have their head above water or their house still underwater, and they're trying to get to stabler ground. So, I think the first rule has to be do no harm. (Applause.)" [2013 National Association of Realtors Conference and Expo, 11/9/13]

Chapter 25

IMMIGRATION

AMERICAN JOBS

Hillary Clinton: "There Has to Be an Extra Effort Made to Try to Fill Jobs with People Who Are Already Here."

"But given the great recession and the fact that so many people lost jobs across the economy including in the tech field, there has to be an extra effort made to try to fill jobs with people who are already here. They can be either native born or immigrants, but already here, so that then if that's not possible you have a good faith argument that you tried, because too many people like the H1B visas are, instead of an opportunity to get good, strong talent, a way of avoiding hiring American workers. So I do think there has to be some sensitivity to that, but I believe that's doable. I don't think that's an overwhelming task." [Hillary Clinton Remarks at Nexenta, 8/28/14]

SECURITY

Clinton: "We've Done a Lot on Border Security, but We Haven't Maybe Done Enough about How We Apply Technology..."

"We've done a lot on border security, but we haven't maybe done enough about how we apply technology so we don't interfere with commerce and recreation and tourism and going back and forth. And representing New York there were a lot of people who lived in New York who were crossing the border all the time." [Remarks for CIBC, 1/22/15]

VISAS

Hillary Clinton Supported H1B Visas.

"But if you look at the evidence, I think the figures are pretty impressive that I think it's like 40 percent of Fortune 500 companies have been started by immigrants. I think obviously the role that immigrants in technology play as evidenced by your hands is just unparalleled. I think that we are hurting ourselves by failing to do comprehensive immigration reform. And I know politically it's difficult because there are a lot of people in public office who hear only the loud voices that are on the negative side, and oftentimes it is out of a place of fear, not a place of understanding or as I'd say evidence. So I think that what we've got to do is keep making the case, but we need more voices. And the only point I would make for the tech community is on the H1B visas, I support them. When I was a Senator from New York I supported them." [Hillary Clinton Remarks at Nexenta, 8/28/14]

Immigration 111

Hillary Clinton Said It Was "Essential to Keep Focused On the Visa Issue" When H1B Visas Were Brought Up.

"PHIL FERNANDEZ: Thank you [...] 40 CEOs said like to a person, H1B, you know, we need more H1Bs. HILLARY CLINTON: Right. [...] So let me just make three quick points. One, I think it's essential to keep focused on the visa issue, because that's a discrete problem that even though I'd like to see it be part of an overall, comprehensive reform, you have to keep pushing to open the aperture, you know, get more and more opportunities." [Hillary Clinton Remarks at Marketo, 4/8/14]

Hillary Clinton Joked "Don't Give" Putin an H1B Visa.

"PHIL FERNANDEZ: I'm just amazed at your ability to talk from income disparity to H1Bs, to Vladmir Putin and everything in-between. HILLARY CLINTON: Don't give him an H1B." [Hillary Clinton Remarks at Marketo, 4/8/14]

Calling for More H1B Visas, Clinton Noted "We Educate People in Our Institutions, and Then We Don't Let Them Stay."

"PRESIDENT JACKSON: Thank you. You know, at SHRM, as HR professionals, we are actively engaged in this debate over comprehensive immigration reform. We see reform as a way to address the projected skills gap that we see in the U.S. Now, your voting record in the Senate indicates a strong support for expanding the H1B Guest Worker Visa Program. What are your thoughts on the immigration reform debate, and where do you think it's headed? MS. HILLARY CLINTON: Well, I hope it's heading toward a new law that will resolve a lot of these hard issues about comprehensive immigration reform. I'm very hopeful that the debate now going on in the Senate that they'll reach a bipartisan agreement, pass a bill and then send it to the House to consider it, and hopefully, the House will pass a comparable bill and then we can work out the differences. It's way overdue. I mean, if you look at what the core of the debate is, yes, we need to make sure we have border security. That's not only about immigration. That's about terrorism, criminal activities, trafficking drugs, people, guns. I mean, there's many reasons to have effective border security in addition to the immigration reasons. We have to do more to bring people out of the shadows, hold employers accountable if they continue to employ people that they know are illegal and put people who are willing to pay their dues literally and figuratively in line for legal status. So I think the bill that the four Republicans and four Democrats came up with has the core principles that we need to enact. I'm sure there will be a lot of variations on amendments, but if the core stays the same, I think that's important. Now, specifically about H1B visas, you know, we give so many more student visas than we give H1B visas. We educate people in our institutions, and then we don't let them stay in our country and work for you and work on behalf of improving our productivity and dealing with our problems. So I know you have advocated strongly for a lot of these reforms. I support what you're trying to do because I think our economic recovery is to some extent fueled by a steady stream of well-qualified, productive workers coming out of our own institutions, native born, legally here and those who have something to contribute who are going to help us continue to grow our economy." [Hillary Clinton remarks at SHRRM Chicago, 6/15/13]

Chapter 26

INCOME INEQUALITY

Clinton: "Even If It May Not Be 100 Percent True, If the Perception Is That Somehow the Game Is Rigged, That Should Be a Problem for All of Us."

"Now, it's important to recognize the vital role that the financial markets play in our economy and that so many of you are contributing to. To function effectively those markets and the men and women who shape them have to command trust and confidence, because we all rely on the market's transparency and integrity. So even if it may not be 100 percent true, if the perception is that somehow the game is rigged, that should be a problem for all of us, and we have to be willing to make that absolutely clear. And if there are issues, if there's wrongdoing, people have to be held accountable and we have to try to deter future bad behavior, because the public trust is at the core of both a free market economy and a democracy." [Clinton Remarks to Deutsche Bank, 10/7/14]

Clinton: "It Is in Everyone's Interest, Most of All Those of You Who Play Such a Vital Role in the Global Economy, to Make Sure That We Maintain, and Where Necessary, Rebuild Trust."

"So it is in everyone's interest, most of all those of you who play such a vital role in the global economy, to make sure that we maintain and where necessary rebuild trust that goes beyond correcting specific instances of abuse of fraud." [Clinton Remarks to Deutsche Bank, 10/7/14]

When Asking about "Wealth Discrepancy" Clinton Discussed the Need to Extend Unemployment Benefits.

MR. IMMELT: Touching again on something you mentioned earlier, this notion of just the wealth discrepancy in the United States, how deep does that run today, and how much of it, you know, do you think can get resolved or be part of a common goal instead of a political divide? MRS. CLINTON: Well, I hope it does because—you know, I'll just take two examples: You know a lot of people who lost their jobs have not been able to find jobs. Now, there's an argument that for some of them their skills are not transferrable, their educational levels are not sufficient, but for many of them there just aren't the jobs yet because a lot of companies have not made the decision to start hiring, which I hope to see, but that's not yet there. So you've got people on long-term unemployment, and it ran out, and the argument for extending it is people have to be kept, number 1, afloat because they have obligations. You know, you don't want to see a cascade where people get behind in house payments and medical payments and school payments or whatever else their obligations might be, but also they have to stay in the job search if they are on long-term unemployment, and I personally think it should be extended. The argument against it is that it creates dependency. Well, I think you can make that argument more effectively when you have 5 percent unemployment instead of over 7 percent and

Income Inequality 115

the real figure, if you counted people who dropped and are no longer seeking work is, you know, above 9 percent. So I think that's just bad economics, and I'd like to see it extended. [Clinton Speech for General Electric's Global Leadership Meeting—Boca Raton, FL, 1/6/14]

Clinton Also Cited the Need to Extend Food Stamp Eligibility.

"The second thing is, you know, cutting food stamps while continuing rather significant payments to certain agricultural interests that produce certain crops. So—you see the articles, you know, billionaire farmer gets crop payments. Food stamps is part of our overall agricultural aid program. So when we cut off food stamps—and the biggest percentage of people on food stamps are children, and what are we proving by doing that? You know, there's always the instance where they find one guy somewhere who misused food stamps. Well, come with me. Come with me into, you know, even neighbors near where I live in Westchester County north of New York City where a lot of immigrants, a lot of, you know, people down on their luck use those food stamps just to try to get through the month, and the House of Representatives is cutting them off. That says a lot to me about what people are actually seeing and feeling. Are we so separate from each other that we don't know that there are people who have a really tough time? Have we just walled ourselves off from those people and have no reason to understand or care about them? Well, I think that's unfortunate because, you know, we need to get back to Henry Ford paying his workers a high wage because he wanted people to buy his cars. You know, economic growth will take off when people in the middle feel more secure again and start spending again." [Clinton Speech for General Electric's Global Leadership Meeting—Boca Raton, FL, 1/6/14]

116   *Christian Mellor*

Clinton Said $51,000 Was "Hard to Live on" in New York City.

"And, so, to me inequality is a morale issue. It certainly is a humanitarian issue, but it's also an economic political issue. And, you know, we just elected a new Mayor in New York City, a lot of controversy because he ran on the tail or two cities. Well, the median income in New York City is $51,000. That's hard to live on, and a lot of people, millions do it, and we ought to be sort of supporting efforts to make sure that people have those ladders of opportunity that somebody like me took advantage of. And, so, inequality to me is the other side of the coin of growth, and we need to do -- we need to take care of both" [Clinton Speech for General Electric's Global Leadership Meeting—Boca Raton, FL, 1/6/14]

Clinton Said Problems like a Stalled Standard of Living Had "Crept up on Us" and "We're All Wondering around Saying, What's Going On, Why Is It Happening?"

CLINTON: So if you look at a recent study that just actually was posted today, if you're in the middle class in Canada, you're better off in general than if you're in the middle class in the United States today. And if you're poorer in the United States, you are worse off than the poor in Canada and Europe. [...] So yeah, we've done some very necessary and good things but we've also, in my view, not adequately addressed the challenges that have come in the last 20, 25 years. They've slowly crept up on us like all of us are the frogs in the giant pot and the heat's been slowly turned up and we haven't jumped out, and if we even started to thinking about it, we weren't sure what we'd find if we did. So we're all wondering around saying, what's going on, why is it happening? And it has certainly economic effects because as people's standard of living stalls, if they believe that their children are not going to be better off—and remember, ever since we have done polling in this country, back to the Great Depression, no matter how poor the vast majority of Americans were, they believed it would be better in the future and they believed it would be better for

Income Inequality 117

their children. That no longer is the case. People are quite concerned that their livelihoods, their lives are not going to get any better, and they're even now worried that neither will their children. So this deserves the kind of thoughtful discussion, not the us versus them, finger pointing, blame placing, because that's not going to get us anywhere, but if we do not address and figure out how we're going to revitalize the middle class and begin the process of once again encouraging more people to rise up, then what I fear is that our politics and our social fabric are going to be dramatically altered. [Clinton Speech for JP Morgan, 4/22/14]

Hillary Clinton Called Rising Inequality a "Troubling Trend Line" and Cited Robert Putnam's Bowling Alone.

"But there's a troubling trend line. The rise of inequality, the decline in recent decades of community organizations and associations memorably documented by Robert Putnam in his book, Bowling Alone, has caused considerable concern about our fraying social fabric, whether or not we still believe in and practice those habits of the heart that were such a hallmark that set us apart from any other part of humanity. Now, this goes way beyond social clubs and certainly beyond bowling teams because in places that are hollowed out by unemployment and economic dislocation, the community networks that provided crucial support to Americans in previous generations are weaker than ever." [Jewish United Fund of Metropolitan Chicago Vanguard Luncheon, 10/28/13]

Matter of Human Nature. Some People Are Going to Figure out a Way to Make a Lot of Money, Sometimes Legally, Sometimes through Corruption or Illegal Activities, but There Are Rich People Everywhere."

"And what we need to do is inject some dynamism and some of good solid economic policies into helping to stabilize the American middle class, because that's really the core of who we are. You know, as I traveled to all those 112 countries, what a big difference that you see in the vast majority of them, there are rich people everywhere. That's just a matter of human nature. Some people are going to figure out a way to make a lot of money, sometimes legally, sometimes through corruption or illegal activities, but there are rich people everywhere. And there are poor people everywhere." [2013 National Association of Realtors Conference and Expo, 11/9/13]

Chapter 27

IRAN

Hillary Clinton Said If Iran Developed a Nuclear Weapon, the Saudis, Emirates, and Egypt Would Try to as Well.

"I have a very simple definition. If they can produce the pieces of it and quickly assemble it, that's a nuclear weapon, even if they keep three different parts of it in different containers somewhere. If they do that it goes back to Lloyd's first point. The Saudis are not going to stand by. They're already trying to figure out how they will get their own nuclear weapons. Then the Emirates are not going to let the Saudis have their own nuclear weapons, and then the Egyptians are going to say: What are we? We're the most important Arab country in the world. We're going to have to have our own nuclear weapons. And then the race is off and we are going to face even worse problems in the region than we currently do today." [Speech to Goldman Sachs, 2013 IBD CEO Annual Conference, 6/4/13]

Hillary Clinton Said the Military Option Was Bombing Iranian Facilities, Not Occupation or Invasion.

"MS. CLINTON: Well, you up the pain that they have to endure by not in any way occupying or invading them but by bombing their facilities. I mean, that is the option. It is not as, we like to say these days, boots on the ground." [Speech to Goldman Sachs, 2013 IBD CEO Annual Conference, 6/4/13]

Hillary Clinton Said There Would Be Unpredictable Consequences to Bombing Iran, Noting It Was a Global Sponsor of Terror.

"MS. CLINTON: They wanted—yeah. But I mean, people will fight for themselves. They will fight for themselves, but this is fighting for a program. I mean, the calculation is exactly as you described it. It's a very hard one, which is why when people just pontificate that, you know, we have no choice. We have to bomb the facilities. They act as though there would be no consequences either predicted or unpredicted. Of course there would be, and you already are dealing with a regime that is the principal funder and supplier of terrorism in the world today" [Speech to Goldman Sachs, 2013 IBD CEO Annual Conference, 6/4/13]

Hillary Clinton Said Iran Has Been Caught Connecting to Terrorism in Bulgaria, Thailand, Cyprus, Kenya, and Even a Plot to Murder the Saudi Ambassador to the US.

"If we had a map up behind us you would be able to see Iranian sponsored terrorism directly delivered by Iranians themselves, mostly through the Revolutionary Guard Corps, the operatives, or through Islah or other proxies from to Latin American to Southeast Asia. They were caught in Bulgaria. They were caught in Cyprus. They were caught in Thailand. They were caught in Kenya. So it's not just against the United States, although they did have that ridiculous plot of finding what they thought was a drug dealer to murder the Saudi ambassador." [Speech to Goldman Sachs, 2013 IBD CEO Annual Conference, 6/4/13]

Iran 121

Hillary Clinton Said Mutually Assured Destruction Did Not Work in the Middle East Because the Gulf States Were Unwilling to Accept a Shared Missile Defense System.

"They really are after the sort of targets of anyone they believe they can terrorize or sort of make pay a price because of policies. So the fact is that there is no good alternative. I mean, people will say, as you do, mutually assured destruction, but that will require the gulf states doing something that so far they've been unwilling to do, which is being part of a missile defense umbrella and being willing to share their defense so that if the best place for radar is somewhere that can then protect the Saudis and the Emirates, the Saudis would have to accept that. That is not likely to happen." [Speech to Goldman Sachs, 2013 IBD CEO Annual Conference, 6/4/13]

Hillary Clinton Said the "Saudis in Particular Are Not Necessarily the Stablest Regimes That You Can Find on the Planet."

"So mutually assured destruction as we had with Europe in the '40s, '50s, '60s, '70s, '80s until the fall of the Soviet Union is much harder to do with the gulf states and it will be unlikely to occur because they will think that they have to defend themselves. And they will get into the business of nuclear weapons, and these are—the Saudis in particular are not necessarily the stablest regimes that you can find on the planet. So it's fraught with all kinds of problems." [Speech to Goldman Sachs, 2013 IBD CEO Annual Conference, 6/4/13]

Hillary Clinton Said People "Get Paid All These Big Bucks for Being in Positions like I Was Just in Trying to Sort It out and Figure out What Is the Smartest Approach for the United States."

"So that's what you get paid all these big bucks for being in positions like I was just in trying to sort it out and figure out what is the smartest approach for the United States and our allies can take that would result in the least amount of danger to ourselves and our allies going forward, a contained Iran or an attacked Iran in the name of

122 Christian Mellor

prevention? And if it were easy somebody else would have figured it out, but it's not. It's a very tough question." [Speech to Goldman Sachs, 2013 IBD CEO Annual Conference, 6/4/13]

Hillary Clinton Said She Believed Rouhani Was Allowed to Be Elected Due to Sanctions but "What They Really Want to Do Is Get Sanction Relief and Give as Little as Possible for That Sanction Relief."

"With respect to the nuclear program, I believe that Rouhani was allowed to be elected by the two major power sources in Iran, the Supreme Leader and the clerics and the Revolutionary Guard led by Suleimani, in part because the sanctions were having a quite damaging effect on the economy, and because of that, there was growing dissatisfaction among the so-called merchant class as well as ordinary consumers and that some action was being demanded. I don't think anyone should have any illusions as to the motives of the Iranian leadership. What they really want to do is get sanction relief and give as little as possible for that sanction relief." [Jewish United Fund of Metropolitan Chicago Vanguard Luncheon, 10/28/13]

"If They Are Not Going to Allow the Missile Program to Be Put under International Control in Some Way, That's a Big Sign of Their Lack of Seriousness, No Matter What They Might Agree to on the Centrifuges."

"And the third issue is their missile program. It doesn't get a lot of discussion. I was with Shimon Peres in the Ukraine a few weeks ago. And he and I were talking about that because the missile program is the delivery vehicle, and if they are not going to allow the missile program to be put under international control in some way, that's a big sign of their lack of seriousness, no matter what they might agree to on the centrifuges." [2014 Jewish United Fund Advance & Major Gifts Dinner, 10/28/13]

Iran 123

Hillary Clinton Said Some Forces in Iran Would Welcome a Military Strike Because It Would Bring Legitimacy to the Regime.

"MS. HILLARY CLINTON: Well, here's the problem because I'm not speaking out of school, but there are forces in Iran that would welcome a military strike because, No. 1, they think a targeted military strike on the facilities that would be known would set back the program maybe a year, maybe two years, but would rally the Iranian people, providing additional legitimacy for the continued rule by the Supreme Leader and the clerics. So, certainly, in the many, many briefings and conversations that I was part of over four years, it's not so clear that there is an absolute fear of a military strike among certain elements within Iran." [2014 Jewish United Fund Advance & Major Gifts Dinner, 10/28/13]

Hillary Clinton Said a Military Strike Could Cause an "Uncontrollable" Reaction and "Could Be a Signal to a Lot of the Neighbors to Take Action against Iranian Assets."

"Now, on the other side, there are those who certainly think it would be very bad. It might cause a reaction on the part of certain elements within Iran that could become uncontrollable. It could be a signal to a lot of the neighbors to take action against Iranian assets. So this is not a very easy message to convey in a way that it causes the kind of reaction that one would want from inside Iran." [2014 Jewish United Fund Advance & Major Gifts Dinner, 10/28/13]

Hillary Clinton Said Sanctions from Congress Weren't Useful outside of International Consensus.

"You know, as somebody who spent a lot of time the first two years putting together those international sanctions, those were very difficult. I mean, we could pass, you know, a million sanctions in the United States Congress. I voted for them when I was a senator. But if you don't have an international consensus on sanctions, you cannot hurt the Iranians the way you need to get their attention to determine whether or

124 *Christian Mellor*

not there is any potential negotiated outcome." [Jewish United Fund of Metropolitan Chicago Vanguard Luncheon, 10/28/13]

Hillary Clinton Said the US Had to Negotiate with Iran on Its Nuclear Program after Rouhani's "Charm Offensive" Because They Had to Maintain the International Consensus on Sanctions.

"So along comes Rouhani who was a nuclear negotiator about ten or so years ago for Iran. He's on a big charm offensive, the new foreign minister is on a big charm offensive. How far he will be able to go given the Supreme Leader and the Revolutionary Guard is not clear yet, but it's very important for us to test that. It's very important for us to engage in the diplomacy that was created by the coercive sanctions for two reasons: First, to really explore in depth what they are willing to do and in return for what; and second, to keep our International Sanctions Coalition together because if the Iranians are on their charm offensive, it's not just with us, it's with the Europeans, it's with the Asians, it's certainly with the Russians and the Chinese. And if they are in a position to be able to say, 'Look, we were prepared to answer a lot of the concerns of the United States and the West, but, of course, the United States wouldn't negotiate with us so we feel like we've done our part so why don't you buy some more oil and gas,' I mean, that's what we have to try to avoid to try to keep them in as tight a position as possible while we test the diplomacy." [Jewish United Fund of Metropolitan Chicago Vanguard Luncheon, 10/28/13]

Chapter 28

ISLAM

Clinton Said Most Muslims Were Peaceful, but "We Can't Close Our Eyes to the Fact That There Is a Distorted and Dangerous Strain of Extremism" Spreading within the Muslim World.

"And I want to be clear, Islam itself is not the adversary. The vast majority of Muslims living here in Canada and the United States are peaceful and tolerant people. We see that every day in our neighborhoods, among those with whom we go to school or work or trade. But we can't close our eyes to the fact that there is a distorted and dangerous strain of extremism within the Muslim world that continues to spread." [Hillary Clinton Remarks for tinePublic—Saskatoon, Canada, 1/21/14]

Chapter 29

ISRAEL

Clinton: "There's That Wonderful Abba Eban Line about How the Palestinians Never Miss an Opportunity to Miss an Opportunity? That Still Seems to Be the Case..."

"The final thing I would say is that within the year that my husband left office, I came home one day and he said, 'You're not going to believe what happened.' And I said, 'What happened?' He said, 'Yasser Arafat called me today, and he said, "You know that deal that you offered us? We've ready to take it now."' And Bill said, 'You know, that president who offered it is no longer president.' So, you know, there's that wonderful Abba Eban line about how the Palestinians never miss an opportunity to miss an opportunity? That still seems to be the case, and the security challenges on all sides now facing Israel are much more acute. So I think it's a heavy lift, but I am very pleased that Secretary Kerry is giving it all he's got to try to get something done." [Clinton Speech for Morgan Stanley, 4/18/13]

Hillary Clinton Said Israel Was Working with Military Government in Egypt and with the Jordanians to Shore up King Abdullah.

"So this is a country in turmoil. In my continuing contact with my, you know, counterparts, my former counterparts, in Israel, I think that they are working hard on the relationship with the new military government in Egypt which is something that's essential for the maintenance of the Camp David Accords and just the day-to-day safety of Israel. They are working closely with the Jordanians because we want to keep, you know, shoring up King Abdullah. And they have, you know, conversations at certain levels going on with others in the region to try to insofar as possible have some coordinated approaches and actions." [Jewish United Fund of Metropolitan Chicago Vanguard Luncheon, 10/28/13]

Hillary Clinton: "One of the Developments of the Arab Spring Is That You Now Have Israel and Saudi Arabia More Closely Aligned in Their Foreign Policy."

"So I think that there's a—and there's a constant effort on the part of the leadership of Israel to make it clear that, you know, they are not going to abide the nuclear program or the terrorist program and to send those messages every day in every way, publicly and privately, to try to influence not just the behavior inside Iran, but increasingly, the larger gulf. I mean, one of the—one of the developments of the Arab spring is that you now have Israel and Saudi Arabia more closely aligned in their foreign policy. MR. ELLIOTT BADZIN: Who would have thunk it?

SECRETARY HILLARY CLINTON: Who would have? And not only about Iran, which they —they both put at the top of their list of concerns, but about Egypt and about Syria and about a lot of other things." [Beth El Synagogue's 13th National Speaker Series, 10/27/13]

Chapter 30

JAPAN

Hillary Clinton Said Japan "Don't Have a Military," and Were Unlikely to Develop Nuclear Weapons Capacity Even in Reaction to North Korea.

"MR. BLANKFEIN: Wouldn't Japan—I mean, isn't the thinking now what is going to happen? But why wouldn't Japan at that point want to have a nuclear capability? MS. CLINTON: Well, that's the problem with these arms races. MR. BLANKFEIN: Nuclear technology —MS. CLINTON: But they don't have a military. They have a currently somewhat questionable and partially defunct civilian nuclear industry. So they would have to make a huge investment, which based on our assessments they don't want to have to make "[Speech to Goldman Sachs, 2013 IBD CEO Annual Conference, 6/4/13]

Hillary Clinton Said the "Mess on the Senkakians" Was Caused by Nationalist Forces in Japan Forcing the Federal Government to Act.

"But there are nationalistic pressures and leaders under the surface in governship and mayor positions who are quite far out there in what they're saying about what Japan should be doing. And part of the reason we're in the mess on the Senkakians is because it had been privately owned. And then the governor of Tokyo wanted to buy them, which would have been a direct provocation to China because it was kind of like: You don't do anything. We don't do anything. Just leave them where they are and don't pay much attention to them. And the prior government in Japan decided: Oh, my gosh. We can't let the governor of Tokyo do this, so we should buy them as the national government." [Speech to Goldman Sachs, 2013 IBD CEO Annual Conference, 6/4/13]

Chapter 31

MARIJUANA

Clinton Said She Was Strongly against Legalizing Marijuana.
"URSULA BURNS: So long means thumbs up, short means thumbs down; or long means I support, short means I don't. I'm going to start with—I'm going to give you about ten long-shorts. SECRETARY CLINTON: Even if you could make money on a short, you can't answer short. URSULA BURNS: You can answer short, but you got to be careful about letting anybody else know that. They will bet against you. So legalization of pot? SECRETARY CLINTON: Short in all senses of the word." [Hillary Clinton Remarks, Remarks at Xerox, 3/18/14]

Chapter 32

MEXICO

Clinton Said She Was Impressed with Enrique Peña Nieto and His Reforms.

"The new leader of Mexico who I didn't have a chance to work with but I'm very impressed by with all of the reforms that he's been able to get through the Mexican legislature he's really done things like reforming the constitution to permit new investments in the Mexican oil company that was previously closed to outside investment, changing education system, doing things that really go hand in hand with what his predecessor was also trying to do." [1/27/14, HWA Remarks at Premier Health]

Chapter 33

MEDIA

Hillary Clinton Praised the Press That Covered Her in the State Department for Being Interested in the Issues.

"So I mean, I am constantly amazed at how attention deficit disordered the political punditry is. Because there is a lot to cover. There is so much that you could actually be educating people about. The difference that I experienced from running for the Senate, being in the Senate, running for president and being Secretary of State is that the press which covered me in the state department were really interested in the issues. I mean, they would drill them. They would have asked a hundred more questions about everything Lloyd has asked in the time that they had with me because they really cared about what I thought, what the US government was doing in these issues." [Speech to Goldman Sachs, 2013 IBD CEO Annual Conference, 6/4/13]

Hillary Clinton: "Our Political Press Has Just Been Captured by Trivia. I Mean, to Me. and so You Don't Want to Give Them Any More Time to Trivialize the Importance of the Issues Than You Have to Give Them."

"Our political press has just been captured by trivia. I mean, to me. And so you don't want to give them any more time to trivialize the importance of the issues than you have to give them. You want to be able to wait as long as possible, because hopefully we will actually see some progress on immigration, for example. Maybe circumstances will force some kind of budget deal. It doesn't look too promising, but stranger things have happened." [Speech to Goldman Sachs, 2013 IBD CEO Annual Conference, 6/4/13]

Chapter 34

NORTH KOREA

Clinton on North Korea: "Right Now, It's Not a Direct Threat to the United States."

MR. BOZZUTO: Well, and—to leave the Middle East but talk about another sponsor of terrorism, my question is really simple. How—how afraid should we be of North Korea? SECRETARY CLINTON: You know, right now, it's not a direct threat to the United States. It is, however, a threat to our treaty allies in South Korea and Japan. It is also a source of instability on the Korean peninsula that could have, you know, ramifications for the region and our interests in the region. [Clinton Speech for National Multi-Housing Council, 4/24/13]

Chapter 35

PERSONAL STORIES

MARINE RECRUITERS

When Asked If in 1975 She Was Rejected from the Marines Because She Was Female, Clinton Said "No" and Explained That They Rejected Her Because She Was "Too Old."

"MR. HOLLADAY: Is it true that until 1975 you applied for the Marines and they told you no because you were a female? MS. HILLARY CLINTON: No. Here is what did happen: It was actually— there was a recruiting station, and I thought, you know, maybe I should consider serving my country by joining the military. So I walked into the recruiting station, and the person on duty was a Marine. And I think I was 26, maybe 27, so, an older potential recruit. I said to the young Marine, I said, 'Well, you know, I'd be interested in getting some information to see whether I could maybe serve. I'm a lawyer. Maybe I could help in some way.' He says, 'Well, I think you are too old for the Marines but maybe the dogs will take you.' I said, 'The dogs?' He goes, 'Yeah, you know, the Army.' I said, 'Well, it doesn't sound like I'm going to be welcome so...'" [American Society for Clinical Pathology Annual Meeting, 9/18/13]

140   *Christian Mellor*

IMMIGRANT GRANDPARENTS

Hillary Clinton Said Her Grandfather Rodham "Came as a Young Boy with His Family to the United States."

"You know, as I briefly described, my father, he, you know, he grew up in Scranton, Pennsylvania. His father came as a young boy with his family to the United States and had two babies and worked in the mills, starting when he was eleven and went until he retired at 65." [Hillary Clinton remarks to ECGR Grand Rapids, 6/17/13]

FATHER'S FOOTBALL SCHOLARSHIP

Hillary Clinton Said Her Father Received a College Football Scholarship.

"And my father played football, so he got a football scholarship to go to college, which was a very good deal, but then he came out of college in the middle of the Depression and there were no jobs. And he heard about a job in Chicago, so he hopped a freight train down to Chicago and got this job, and it was serving as a representative selling drapery fabrics around the Upper Midwest, probably came to Grand Rapids back then." [Hillary Clinton remarks to ECGR Grand Rapids, 6/17/13]

Hillary Clinton Stated Her Father Made It to College on a Football Scholarship.

"My father made it to college on a football scholarship, started a small business, my mother overcame a childhood of abandonment to help build a middle class life for me and my brothers and I knew I was a beneficiary not only of their love and hard work, but their aspirations for us and a larger community that believed as they did in America's promise." [0224015 HWA Remarks for Watermark (Santa Clara CA).docx, p. 8]

Chapter 36

PERSONAL WEALTH

Hillary Clinton: "I'm Kind of Far Removed" from the Struggles of the Middle Class "Because the Life I've Lived and the Economic, You Know, Fortunes That My Husband and I Now Enjoy."

"And I am not taking a position on any policy, but I do think there is a growing sense of anxiety and even anger in the country over the feeling that the game is rigged. And I never had that feeling when I was growing up. Never. I mean, were there really rich people, of course there were. My father loved to complain about big business and big government, but we had a solid middle class upbringing. We had good public schools. We had accessible health care. We had our little, you know, one-family house that, you know, he saved up his money, didn't believe in mortgages. So I lived that. And now, obviously, I'm kind of far removed because the life I've lived and the economic, you know, fortunes that my husband and I now enjoy, but I haven't forgotten it." [Hillary Clinton Remarks at Goldman-Black Rock, 2/4/14]

The Moderator Joked That It Was Said Hillary Clinton Was Going to Do a Lot of Speeches When She Left the State Department.

"JIM GREENWOOD: All right. The day is young. So when you left State, it was said that you were going to do beaches and speeches. SEC. HILLARY CLINTON: Right. JIM GREENWOOD: I've been watching television. You've been doing a lot of speeches. Doing any beaches? SEC. HILLARY CLINTON: Not yet. Not yet." [06252014 HWA Remarks at BIO (San Diego, CA).docx, p. 1]

Chapter 37

PIVOT TO ASIA

Clinton Said She Worried That the United States Would Not "Maintain That Continuity of Attention and Support That Is Needed in Asia and Elsewhere," as They Had to Build South Korean Democracy after the Korean War.

"And think about what they went through. I mean, South Korea has coups, have assassinations, have, you know, really terrible politics for a very long time. They didn't become what we would consider a functional democracy overnight, but we never gave up. We had troops there, we had aid there, we had a presence of American business there. We were there for the long run. And what I worry about is that in a time of shrinking resources and well-deserved demands that we pay attention here at home to what's happening to the American people, that we're not going to maintain that continuity of attention and support that is needed in Asia and elsewhere. So I'm hoping that it, you know, certainly is maintained despite the hiccups, but it takes time and resources to do that." [Goldman Sachs AIMS Alternative Investments Symposium, 10/24/13]

Chapter 38

POLITICS

Hillary Clinton Noted the Gang of 8, Which Included Marco Rubio, as How the Legislative Process Is Supposed to Work on Immigration.

"This is the way the legislative process is supposed to work on immigration. You have four republicans, four democrats, they worked very hard to reach consensus. There was an actual markup of the bill. The judiciary committee, they actually proposed amendments and voted on them, but they had made a deal that they would stick with their basic outlines of their proposal and now they're debating it on the floor of the senate." [06242013 Remarks at KKR Los Angeles.doc, p. 28]

Clinton: "If You're on the Left, the Best Way to Get Rid of You Is by Having Somebody Even Further Left Run against You in a Primary, and the Same If You're on the Right, Having Somebody Even Further Right."

CLINTON: I mean, one of our great problems right now is nobody wants to be around people they disagree with. They just kind of write them off. Everybody watches TV that reinforces your already existing prejudices, and, you know, that's how we're kind of dividing ourselves

146   *Christian Mellor*

up, and so we've created a House of Representatives where, if you're on the left, the best way to get rid of you is by having somebody even further left run against you in a primary, and the same if you're on the right, having somebody even further right. So there's no incentive in so many of our districts for people to compromise because they're afraid that if they disappoint or anger their supporters that they'll put in somebody to run against them in a primary. But that's our fault. I mean, we let that happen because, you know, we don't really stand up and say, wait a minute, that's not in the interests of the whole. [Clinton Speech For National Multi-Housing Council, 4/24/13]

Clinton: "I'm a Big Believer in Balance on Nearly Any Issue..."

MR. BOZZUTO: The—you and I and Doug talked briefly in the hallway about how apartments are becoming increasingly attractive to young people and older people, and yet we have a housing policy that I will say discriminates against renters through the mortgage interest deduction. How—how should we create a more balanced housing policy that doesn't discriminate against one group of people? SECRETARY CLINTON: Well, "balanced" is the right word. I think that, you know—from the, you know, the little bit that I know—you all are the experts—we're going to need even more rental housing. It is, as you say, sort of the, you know, the Boomers plus the Echo Boomers plus people who have been priced out of or forced out of home ownership, and there has to be a balance. I'm—I'm a big believer in balance on nearly any issue, and I guess I would say just three things. [Clinton Speech for National Multi-Housing Council, 4/24/13]

Clinton: "But If Everybody's Watching, You Know, All of the Back Room Discussions and the Deals, You Know, Then People Get a Little Nervous, to Say the Least. So, You Need Both a Public and a Private Position."

CLINTON: You just have to sort of figure out how to—getting back to that word, "balance"—how to balance the public and the private efforts that are necessary to be successful, politically, and that's not just a comment about today. That, I think, has probably been true for all of our history, and if you saw the Spielberg movie, Lincoln, and how he was maneuvering and working to get the 13th Amendment passed, and he called one of my favorite predecessors, Secretary Seward, who had been the governor and senator from New York, ran against Lincoln for president, and he told Seward, I need your help to get this done. And Seward called some of his lobbyist friends who knew how to make a deal, and they just kept going at it. I mean, politics is like sausage being made. It is unsavory, and it always has been that way, but we usually end up where we need to be. But if everybody's watching, you know, all of the back room discussions and the deals, you know, then people get a little nervous, to say the least. So, you need both a public and a private position. And finally, I think—I believe in evidence-based decision making. I want to know what the facts are. I mean, it's like when you guys go into some kind of a deal, you know, are you going to do that development or not, are you going to do that renovation or not, you know, you look at the numbers. You try to figure out what's going to work and what's not going to work. [Clinton Speech for National Multi-Housing Council, 4/24/13]

Clinton Criticized Those Who Run for Office as "Kind of above That Political Process, the Democratic Process."
"So when somebody runs for and asks for your vote who tries to set him or herself kind of above that political process, the democratic process, that person should not earn your vote. And in addition, they should not earn your contribution." [Remarks to CME Group, 11/18/13]

Hillary Clinton Said Moderate Voices in Congress Need More Support, Citing Eight-Senator Immigration Compromise.
"So we got to make sure that we begin listening to each other, we begin to reward people who try to make the tough decisions in the

middle like these eight senators on immigration for republicans and for democrats. You know, they've got to be given support because they're trying to solve a real problem, and then we have to keep looking for more and more ways to do that as well." [Hillary Clinton remarks to Apollo Global Management, 5/13/13]

Clinton Compared the Retail Industry to Politics: "We Have to Know What's on People's Minds If You're Going to Sell Them Something or Get Their Vote."

"You know, it was a retail business obviously, and retailing is a lot like politics, you have very direct relationships with your customers or with your voters, we have to know what's on people's minds if you're going to sell them something or get their vote. And I learned a lot from, you know, watching how he managed this growing company, how he dealt with his associates, you know, they would have the annual meeting in the field house of the University of Arkansas basketball arena, so you have tens of thousands of people, you'd have entertainment and they'd bus in, you know, these men and women who worked at Walmarts from all over the country and build camaraderie and basically kind of you're on the Walmart team." [Hillary Clinton remarks at Sanford Bernstein, 5/29/13]

Clinton Said That Both the Democratic and Republican Parties Should Be "Moderate."

"URSULA BURNS: Interesting. Democrats? SECRETARY CLINTON: Oh, long, definitely. URSULA BURNS: Republicans? SECRETARY CLINTON: Unfortunately, at the time, short. URSULA BURNS: Okay. We'll go back to questions. SECRETARY CLINTON: We need two parties. URSULA BURNS: Yeah, we do need two parties. SECRETARY CLINTON: Two sensible, moderate, pragmatic parties." [Hillary Clinton Remarks, Remarks at Xerox, 3/18/14]

Politics 149

Hillary Clinton Blamed Gerrymandering for Rewarding Partisanship.

"Secondly, you know, people get rewarded for being partisan, and that's on both sides. The biggest threat that Democrats and Republicans face today, largely because of gerrymandering in the House, is getting a primary opponent from either the far right or the far left." [Speech to Goldman Sachs, 2013 IBD CEO Annual Conference, 6/4/13]

Hillary Clinton Said There Was a State Senator Who Had a Rating from the NRA Who Still Lost Their Support Because She Didn't Support One Gun Rights Bill.

"You know, there is no reason you would have noticed this, but there was a woman in the Senate—and I think it was Kentucky—recently who had an A plus rating from the NRA. A plus rating. She was a country legislator, highly regarded, and she was a chairman of a committee in the state legislature. And somebody introduced a bill with—you know, it's not too much exaggeration to say that you should have your gun in your car at all times and it should be visible. And she said: Let's table it for a minute and think about the consequences. So the NRA recruited an opponent for her who beat her. They put a lot of money into it and basically: You couldn't be reasonable. You couldn't say let's try to reason this out together. You had to toe the line, and whether it's a financial line or gun control line or whatever the line might be. But people let that happen. Voters let that happen." [Speech to Goldman Sachs, 2013 IBD CEO Annual Conference, 6/4/13]

Hillary Clinton Said in Hong Kong Business Leaders Asked Her If the US Would Default on Its Debt.

"And I was in Hong Kong in the summer of 2011 and I had a preexisting program with a big business group there, and before we had a reception and there were about a hundred business leaders, many of them based in Hong Kong, some of them from mainland China, some of them from Singapore and elsewhere. They were lining up and saying to

150 *Christian Mellor*

me: Is it true that the American Congress might default on America's full faith and credit, their standing, that you won't pay your bills? And you know I'm sitting there I'm representing all of you. I said: Oh, no. No. 26 No. That's just politics. We'll work it through. And I'm sitting there: Oh, boy. I hope that is the case." [Speech to Goldman Sachs, 2013 IBD CEO Annual Conference, 6/4/13]

Hillary Clinton Pointed to the Gang of Eight Senators on Immigration as an Example of Productive Compromise.

"I've been an elected official, an appointed official. There is nothing easy about working toward a compromise. I give a lot of credit to the eight senators, four Republicans and four Democrats in the Senate. You go from very conservative to what we would call very liberal. And they have sat down and they hammered out a compromise, and then they made a pledge they would stick to it as it went through the regular order of the committee hearing. How unusual. "[Speech to Goldman Sachs, 2013 IBD CEO Annual Conference, 6/4/13]

Hillary Clinton: "If You Are Not Willing to Be Active in Your Democracy and Do What Is Necessary to Deal with Our Problems, I Think You Should Be Voted Out."

"And I don't care if you're a liberal icon or a conservative icon. If you are not willing to be active in your democracy and do what is necessary to deal with our problems, I think you should be voted out. I think you should just be voted out, and I would like to see more people saying that." [Speech to Goldman Sachs, 2013 IBD CEO Annual Conference, 6/4/13]

Hillary Clinton Said Gerrymandering Gives Politicians "No Incentive to Try to Make the Tough Decisions."

"So I do think that the positions have hardened in the last years; that a number of the districts in the House that were gerrymandered to be safe districts for incumbents or for at least parties are filled with people

Politics 151

who have nothing to fear from taking a reasonable, responsible position and everything to fear from somebody being put in with a lot of money to their right and having a primary against them. So they get no incentive to try to make the tough decisions." [2014 Jewish United Fund Advance & Major Gifts Dinner, 10/28/13]

Hillary Clinton Said the Country Was in a "Worse Position Than We Were in the '90s."

"We'll see whether we can get to a resolution just on the budget and then see whether there is any appetite that permits a broader negotiation like what we had in Bill's second term that—you know, look, I can't help saying it. If we had stuck with that economic policy, we wouldn't have deficits, and we would have considerably paid down our debt, but we had two wars, 9-11 and a very significant double tax cut at a time when we couldn't really afford the tax cut because of what other obligations we had. So now we are in a worse position than we were in the '90s. So it's going to be even more important to have a very clear path set forward that people not only follow internally but begin to make the external cases to leaders in business and other institutional influencers across the country to put pressure on the Congress to get to do exactly what you said, try to negotiate a more comprehensive agreement that will be good for the economy and good for our global leadership." [2014 Jewish United Fund Advance & Major Gifts Dinner, 10/28/13]

Hillary Clinton Called for Reform of Senate Rules to Allow More Up and Down Votes.

"You know, I really have come to believe that we need to change the rules in the Senate, having served there for eight years. It's only gotten more difficult to do anything. And I think nominees deserve a vote up or down. Policies deserve a vote up or down. And I don't think that a small handful of senators should stand in the way of that, because, you know, a lot of those senators are really obstructionist.

They should get out. They should make their case. They should go ahead and debate. But they shouldn't be able to stop the action of the United States Senate. So I think there does have to be some reworking of the rules, particularly in the Senate." [Goldman Sachs Builders and Innovators Summit, 10/29/13]

Hillary Clinton Praised California's Adoption of Non-Partisan Redistricting.

"I think that, as has been discussed many times, the partisan drawing of lines in Congressional districts gives people—gives incumbents certainly a lot more protection than an election should offer. And then they're only concerned about getting a challenge from the left of the Democratic Party or a challenge from the right in the Republican Party. And they're not representing really the full interests of the people in the area that they're supposed to be. California moved toward this non-partisan board, and I think there should be more efforts in states to do that and get out of the ridiculous gerrymandering that has given us so many members who don't really care what is happening in the country, don't really care what the facts are. They just care whether they get a primary opponent." [Goldman Sachs Builders and Innovators Summit, 10/29/13]

Hillary Clinton Praised Lamar Alexander for Standing against Tea Party Extremism.

"SECRETARY CLINTON: Yeah. You want them to prove it by saying, you know, we're going to act differently in our voting and our giving. And it could make a very big difference.

Now, some of the Republicans are also fighting back. I mean, somebody like Lamar Alexander, who's been a governor and a senator of Tennessee, and they're mounting a Tea Party challenge against him. He's going right at it. He is not afraid to take them on. And more moderate Republicans have to do that as well. Take back their party from the extremists and the obstructionists." [Goldman Sachs Builders and Innovators Summit, 10/29/13]

Lloyd Blankfein Joked "I'm Proud That the Financial Services Industry Has Been the One Unifying Theme That Binds Everybody Together in Common."

"So it's important that people speak out and stand up against it, and especially people who are Republicans, who say, look, that's not the party that I'm part of. I want to get back to having a two-party system that can have an adult conversation and a real debate about the future. MR. BLANKFEIN: Yeah, and one thing, I'm glad—I'm proud that the financial services industry has been the one unifying theme that binds everybody together in common. (Laughter.)" [Goldman Sachs Builders and Innovators Summit, 10/29/13]

Hillary Clinton Said She Would like to "See More Successful Business People Run for Office" Because they Have a "Certain Level of Freedom."

"SECRETARY CLINTON: That's a really interesting question. You know, I would like to see more successful business people run for office. I really would like to see that because I do think, you know, you don't have to have 30 billion, but you have a certain level of freedom. And there's that memorable phrase from a former member of the Senate: You can be maybe rented but never bought. And I think it's important to have people with those experiences. And especially now, because many of you in this room are on the cutting edge of technology or health care or some other segment of the economy, so you are people who look over the horizon. And coming into public life and bringing that perspective as well as the success and the insulation that success gives you could really help in a lot of our political situations right now." [Goldman Sachs Builders and Innovators Summit, 10/29/13]

154   *Christian Mellor*

Hillary Clinton Said There Was "a Bias against People Who Have Led Successful And/Or Complicated Lives," Citing the Need to Divest of Assets, Positions, and Stocks.

"SECRETARY CLINTON: Yeah. Well, you know what Bob Rubin said about that. He said, you know, when he came to Washington, he had a fortune. And when he left Washington, he had a small --MR. BLANKFEIN: That's how you have a small fortune, is you go to

Washington. SECRETARY CLINTON: You go to Washington. Right. But, you know, part of the problem with the political situation, too, is that there is such a bias against people who have led successful and/or complicated lives. You know, the divestment of assets, the stripping of all kinds of positions, the sale of stocks. It just becomes very onerous and unnecessary." [Goldman Sachs Builders and Innovators Summit, 10/29/13]

Hillary Clinton Called the Confirmation Process "Absurd."

"MR. BLANKFEIN: Confirmation. SECRETARY CLINTON: The confirmation process is absurd. And it drives out a lot of people. So, yes, we would like to see people, but it's a heavy price for many to pay and maybe not one that they're ready to pay." [Goldman Sachs Builders and Innovators Summit, 10/29/13]

Chapter 39

PRO-FREE TRADE

Hillary Clinton Said the United States Believes in an Open and Free System in the Global Economy.

"Now, these policies run directly counter to the values and principles that the United States has worked for many decades to embed in the global economy. We believe in an open, free, transparent and fair system, with clear rules of the road, that benefit everybody, a real competition. But I have to say that not just the Chinese and the Russians, but others believe in something else altogether. So faced with this challenge, we could choose to continue fighting for individual American companies like Corning and FedEx, and I certainly did that throughout my time as secretary, but given the scope of the threats to the global economy I thought we needed to think bigger." [06262014 HWA Remarks for GTCR (Chicago, IL).docx, p. 4]

Hillary Clinton Said She Made the Argument for Openness in Trade since American and Foreign Manufacturers Wanted Access to Markets Oversees.

"I thought I was doing pretty well. I'm making the case, making the argument for openness, fairness, transparency, claiming, look, Malaysia manufacturers want access to markets overseas as much as American manufacturers, Indian firms want fair treatment when they invest abroad, just as we do, Chinese artists want to protect their creations from piracy, every society seeking to develop a strong research and technology sector needs intellectual property protection to make trade fair as well as freer. Developing countries have to do a better job of improving productivity, raising labor conditions, and protecting the environment, on and on." [06262014 HWA Remarks for GTCR (Chicago, IL).docx, p. 5]

Hillary Clinton Said That the United States Saw Fewer Jobs with Greater Competition with Free Trade but Thoughtful Policies in the 1990s Saw an Economic Boom.

"But certainly increasing productivity, fewer jobs is the simplest, greater competition from abroad as the world began to really open up and I think there was a reversal to some extent fueled by technology but also fueled by thoughtful policies in the 90's where there was this, you know, economic boom that created 22 million new jobs and lots of people, you know, took advantage of that." [05162013 Remarks to Banco Itau.doc, p. 44-45]

Hillary Clinton Said That She's All for Free Trade, but She's Also for Reciprocity.

"Now I'm all for trade, I'm all for free trade but I'm also all for a reciprocity and a lot of times that is not coming back at us, you know, probably the single biggest source of complaints that I began fielding from American businesses the last year was how they were being squeezed in countries like China, you know, companies that had been there ten, 20 years even, pioneering companies, you know, they were coming to me and saying, you know, I had these deals and now all of a sudden state enterprise X is telling me, you know, we're not going to renew your license for that. So, if you are going to have the rules of the free market it's really in American interest to make sure that everybody

Pro-Free Trade

follows those rules. So, yes, does trade sometimes get distorted, to the detriment of a country like ours, yes. In general we remain the most open market but in particular we may have to send some messages and I think that's smart, you know, strategic planning and messaging." [05162013 Remarks to Banco Itau.doc, p. 46-47]

Hillary Clinton Said Her Dream Is a Hemispheric Common Market, with Open Trade and Open Markets.

"My dream is a hemispheric common market, with open trade and open borders, sometime in the future with energy that is as green and sustainable as we can get it, powering growth and opportunity for every person in the hemisphere." [05162013 Remarks to Banco Itau.doc, p. 28]

Hillary Clinton Said We Have to Have a Concerted Plan to Increase Trade; We Have to Resist Protectionism and Other Kinds of Barriers to Trade.

"Secondly, I think we have to have a concerted plan to increase trade already under the current circumstances, you know, that Inter-American Development Bank figure is pretty surprising. There is so much more we can do, there is a lot of low hanging fruit but businesses on both sides have to make it a priority and it's not for governments to do but governments can either make it easy or make it hard and we have to resist, protectionism, other kinds of barriers to market access and to trade and I would like to see this get much more attention and be not just a policy for a year under president X or president Y but a consistent one." [05162013 Remarks to Banco Itau.doc, p. 32]

Hillary Clinton Said "Just Think of What Doubling the Trade between the United States and Latin America Would Mean for Everyone in This Room."

"Just think of what doubling the trade between the United States and Latin America would mean for everybody in this room and it

158   *Christian Mellor*

doesn't happen by accident, it happens because people get up every day and decide they're going to make an effort." [05162013 Remarks to Banco Itau.doc, p. 14]

Hillary Clinton Praised TPP.

"Greater connections in our own hemisphere hold such promise. The United States and Canada are working together with a group of open market democracies along the Pacific Rim, Mexico, Colombia, Peru, Chile, to expand responsible trade and economic cooperation." [Canada 2020 Speech, 10/6/14]

Clinton: "People at the Heart of the Private Sector Need to Keep Making the Argument That a More Open, Resilient Economic System Will Create More Broadly Shared Prosperity."

"I think we all, not just public officials or outside analysts, but people at the heart of the private sector need to keep making the argument that a more open, resilient economic system will create more broadly shared prosperity than state capitalism, petro-capitalism or crony capitalism ever will." [Clinton Remarks to Deutsche Bank, 10/7/14]

Hillary Clinton: "We Could Do a Whole Lot More Business with Our Neighbors to the North and the South."

"And I want to underscore that point. We could do a whole lot more business with our neighbors to the north and the south. They are our biggest customers right now. And we need to be paying more attention as to how we build economic relationships in this hemisphere, a hemisphere that is now is largely—not completely—but largely democratic, largely free-market economies where we actually now export more and import more from than most people, most Americans

Pro-Free Trade 159

know." [Hillary Clinton Remarks at the International Dairy-DeliBakery Association, 6/2/14]

Clinton Noted Unfair Chinese Trade Practices against Corning by Imposing a 17% Tariff on Their Products.

"Corning, a company in Upstate New York was the inventor of Gorilla Glass, which supplies not only fiber optics, but other important products all over the world to Apple, to Samsung, to so many, had been in China in the fiber optics business for a long time and basically the Chinese showed up and said we think you're dumping, we're imposing a 17 percent tariff, which would have effectively put them out of business, unless you go into a joint agreement with company X over here. And that was the surest way to lose your intellectual property and your trade secrets and all the rest." [Remarks to eBay, 3/11/15]

Clinton Touted the Importance of Trade with Asia, Said "I Led the Way on This, That We Were Going to Be a Major Presence" in Asia.

"One, we created the Asia-Pacific Economic Community where a lot of economic issues are hashed out, you know, tariffs and the like. And the other which we joined during the first term of the Obama Administration, something called the East Asia Summit. Now, why do I tell you that? Because 40 percent of all of America's and the world's trade goes through the South China Sea; because we have defense treaties with five nations, Japan, Korea, Thailand, the Philippines, Australia; because we are in a competition for the future and we need more partners and fewer adversaries. So we decided, and I led the way on this, that we were going to be a major presence, because for the previous eight years, understandably we've been focused on South Asia and the Middle East, almost to the exclusion of Asia." [Remarks to New York Tri-State of the Market, 11/14/13]

160   *Christian Mellor*

Hillary Clinton Said Scrap Recycling Demand from Asia Was Helping Improve Our Trade Balance and Fuel Our Economic Recovery.

"I'm also delighted to learn that scrap products are a key export for the United States. By helping meet the demands for raw materials from emerging economies in Asia and elsewhere, you're improving our trade balance and fueling our economic recovery. We're talking about 20 to 30 billion in exports every year. And I looked at the program for this conference and was fascinated by all of the different issues that that leads you to study and learn about." [Hillary Clinton Remarks at the Institute of Scrap Recycling Industries Convention, 4/10/14]

Hillary Clinton: "Our Future Growth Will Get a Real Shot in the Arm If We Reach Farther into the Burgeoning Consumer Markets across" Asia-Pacific Region.

"More than half the world's population lives in the vast region from the Indian Ocean to the Island Nations. Here we find some of our most trusted allies and valuable trading partners, many of the world's most dynamic trade and energy routes. A few years ago, when our country was struggling through the worst economic downturn since the Great Depression, American exports to the Asia-Pacific helped spur our recovery. Our future growth will get a real shot in the arm if we reach farther into the burgeoning consumer markets across the region. [...] And you are on track here in this state, in this city to take full advantage of a 21st century economy, and to help make sure that the United States remains a strong presence and a power in the Pacific." [Hillary Clinton Remarks at the World Affairs Council of Oregon, 4/8/14]

Clinton: "The United States and Canada Are Working Together with a Group of Open Market Democracies along the Pacific Rim [...] to Expand Responsible Trade and Economic Cooperation."

"The middle class in Latin America has roughly doubled since 2000, including big increases in Brazil and Mexico. That translates into

Pro-Free Trade 161

increased prosperity for them and more than 50 million new middle class consumers eager to buy U.S. and Canadian goods and services. That's why the United States and Canada are working together with a group of open market democracies along the Pacific Rim—Mexico, Colombia, Peru and Chile—to expand responsible trade and economic cooperation." [Remarks for CIBC, 1/22/15]

Clinton: "The North American Future That I Imagine Is One That Would [...] Give Us a Much More Open Border Where Goods and Services More Easily Flowed..."

"The North American future that I imagine is one that would give us energy connectivity, give us a much more open border where goods and services more easily flowed, would give us the chance to put our heads together about what else we can do together, bringing Mexico in to continue the work we have started on health care like early warning systems for epidemic diseases. We saw that in 2009 with the spread of a particularly virulent form of the flu that first came to our part of the world and Mexico, and because of the cooperation, because of the investments we made, were able to stop it in its tracks." [Remarks for CIBC, 1/22/15]

Clinton: "When My Husband Was Elected in His First Two Years He Made a Lot of Changes. [...] He Passed NAFTA, Alienating a Lot of the Democratic Base."

"But, I think it's important to go back just for another historic minute. When my husband was elected in his first two years he made a lot of changes. And he passed a tax program to try to get us out of the deficit and debt situation that we were mired in after 12 years of quadrupling the debt. He passed really strong gun control laws, taking on the NRA, no easy matter to do in American politics. He passed NAFTA, alienating a lot of the Democratic base. We fought for healthcare reform unsuccessfully." [Remarks for CIBC, 1/22/15]

Clinton: "It Was a Good Sign When Prime Minister Abe Said That Japan Would Negotiate on the Transpacific Partnership."

"And some of you are experts, which I certainly am not, on the Japanese economy, if the prime minister and his government will now willing to open up the internal market and incentivizing these changes and taking on the tough political hurdles, I think you could see sustainable growth. At what level, I can't predict, but it was a good sign when Prime Minister Abe said that Japan would negotiate on the Transpacific partnership, that is something that we tried to get prior prime ministers to commit to, and they were under pressure from the car industry and from the rice farmers and others, but he did say Japan wants to be part of the TPP. If they follow through on that that will be a good sign." [Hillary Clinton remarks at Sanford Bernstein, 5/29/13]

Hillary Clinton Said She "Strongly Supported" Trade and Regulatory Harmonization with Europe, Pointing to French Agriculture as a Stumbling Block.

"But on the trade and regulatory harmonization, we are very serious about that and something that I strongly supported. The discussions are ongoing. It will come down, as it often does, to agriculture, particularly French agriculture, and we'll just have to see how much we can get done by that process. And there is no doubt that if we can make progress on the trade regulatory front it would be good for the Europeans. It would be good for us. And I would like to see us go as far as we possibly can with a real agreement, not a phony agreement. You know, the EU signs agreements all the time with nearly everybody, but they don't change anything. They just kind of sign them and see what comes of it" [Speech to Goldman Sachs, 2013 IBD CEO Annual Conference, 6/4/13]

Pro-Free Trade 163

Hillary Clinton Said We Had "an Opportunity to Really Actually Save Money in Our Respective Regulatory Schemes, Increase Trade with the TPC."

I think we have an opportunity to really actually save money in our respective regulatory schemes, increase trade not only between ourselves but also be more effective in helping to keep the world on a better track for a rural spaced global trading system by having us kind of set the standards for that, along with the TPC, which we didn't mention when we talked about Asia, which I think is also still proceeding." [Speech to Goldman Sachs, 2013 IBD CEO Annual Conference, 6/4/13]

Chapter 40

REDUCING REGULATIONS

Clinton: "How Do We Strengthen and Improve Our Financial Systems to Promote Responsible Investments While Preventing Irresponsible Risk-Taking? I'm a Huge Supporter of Risk-Taking."

"How do we strengthen and improve our financial systems to promote responsible investments while preventing irresponsible risk-taking? I'm a huge supporter of risk-taking. I've kind of done a little bit of that in my life. And there are lots of ways of doing it. But I don't believe that risk-taking should be subsidized. I think we have to figure out how we strike the right balance." [Remarks for CIBC, 1/22/15]

Hillary Clinton: "You Know, I'm Not in the Pro- or Anti-Regulation Camp, I'm in the Smart Regulation Camp."

HILLARY CLINTON: "And we need to do more to be sensible about regulation. You know, I'm not in the pro- or anti-regulation camp, I'm in the smart regulation camp. I mean, what works, what doesn't work, get rid of what doesn't work and be willing to work with businesses on that. You know, obviously, when I was a senator, I had great working relationships with, you know, most of the businesses and their associations in New York because I listened. And I think there is a perception that maybe that is not as common as it needs to be in our party." [Hillary Clinton Remarks at Council of Insurance Agents and Brokers, 10/13/14]

Clinton Said She Had "Great Working Relationships with [...] Most of the Businesses and Their Associations in New York."

HILLARY CLINTON: "You know, obviously, when I was a senator, I had great working relationships with, you know, most of the businesses and their associations in New York because I listened. And I think there is a perception that maybe that is not as common as it needs to be in our party." [Hillary Clinton Remarks at Council of Insurance Agents and Brokers, 10/13/14]

Chapter 41

REFUGEES

Hillary Clinton Used the Experience of Cuban Prisoners in Fort Smith Arkansas to Illustrate the Complexity of Civilian vs Military Rule.

"I think that the civilian rule has served us well, and I don't want to do anything that upsets it even though I have a very personal experience. You remember when Castro opened the prisons and sent all the criminals to the United States? MR. BLANKFEIN: The—MS. CLINTON: A lot of those prisoners were ordered to go to a fort in Ft. Smith, Arkansas, Ft. Chaffee, and my husband was governor of Arkansas at the time. It was a military fort, so the United States military ran it. So if you were on the fort you were under US military authority, but if you stepped off the fort you were not. And the result was there was a riot where prisoners were breaking through the gates, and the US military would not stop them." [Speech to Goldman Sachs, 2013 IBD CEO Annual Conference, 6/4/13]

Hillary Clinton: "We Do Not Ever Want to Turn over to Our Military the Kind of Civilian Authority That Should Be Exercised by Elected Officials."

"So my husband as governor had to call out the state police. So you had the military inside basically saying under the law we can't do anything even to stop prisoners from Cuba. So it is complicated, but it's complicated in part for a reason, because we do not ever want to turn over to our military the kind of civilian authority that should be exercised by elected officials. So I think that's the explanation." [Speech to Goldman Sachs, 2013 IBD CEO Annual Conference, 6/4/13]

Chapter 42

RUSSIA

Hillary Clinton Stated What She Said Yesterday Is That Claims by Putin and Other Russians That They Had to Go into Crimea Was Reminiscent of Germany in the 1930s.

"What I said yesterday is that the claims by President Putin and other Russians that they had to go into Crimea and maybe further into Eastern Ukraine because they had to protect the Russian minorities. And that is reminiscent of claims that were made back in the 1930s when Germany under the Nazis kept talking about how they had to protect German minorities in Poland, in Czechoslovakia, and elsewhere throughout Europe. So I just want everybody to have a little historic perspective. I'm not making a comparison, certainly, but I am recommending that we, perhaps, can learn from this tactic that has been used before." [03052014 HWA Remarks at UCLA.DOC, p. 19]

On Missile Defense, Clinton Said, "We Don't Believe That There Will Be a Threat from Russia."

"I last saw [Putin] in Vladivostok where I represented President Obama in September for the Asia Pacific economic community. I sat next to him. He's an engaging and, you know, very interesting

170   *Christian Mellor*

conversationalist. We talked about a lot of issues that were not the hot-button issues between us, you know, his view on missile defense, which we think is misplaced because, you know, we don't believe that there will be a threat from Russia, but we think that both Russia and the United States are going to face threats from their perimeter, either from rogue states like Iran or from terrorist groups, that's not the way he sees it." [Hillary Clinton remarks at Sanford Bernstein, 5/29/13]

Clinton: "but Nobody Doubted, or at Least I'll Speak for Myself, I Never Doubted That Putin Still Basically Made the Decisions."

CLINTON: So when President Obama took office and I became Secretary of State, the President at the time was Dmitry Medvedev, who was installed by Putin, and he was much easier to get along with. He had a more modern view of what Russia could become. But nobody doubted, or at least I'll speak for myself, I never doubted that Putin still basically made the decisions. So when Putin decided he wanted to be president again in the fall of 2011, it was this awkward thing, where big rally, Medvedev gets up and says, oh, I'm so happy Putin wants to come back as president. I'll be prime minister. The whole thing was staged. It was pretty much of a charade. And then they had parliamentary elections in December 2011. In the meantime, we knew that they had that brutal crackdown in Chechnya. They were beginning to really pressure the press and dissidents, and anyone who considered themselves an opposition leader. So there was a lot going on internally in Russia. But then in December 2011, they had parliamentary elections, which were fraudulent, and clearly illegitimate. And I was Secretary, so I said, you know, we're concerned by what we see as irregularities in the voting in Russia, et cetera. And then he attacked me personally, and people were pouring into the streets in Moscow and St. Petersburg to protest, and Putin was attacking me. And he basically said I had made them go out and protest against him. [Clinton Speech at UConn, 4/23/14]

Russia   171

Hillary Clinton Said She "Would Love It If We Could Continue to Build a More Positive Relationship with Russia."

"And finally on Afghanistan and Russia. Look, I would love it if we could continue to build a more positive relationship with Russia. I worked very hard on that when I was Secretary, and we made some progress with Medvedev, who was president in name but was obviously beholden to Putin, but Putin kind of let him go and we helped them get into the WTO for several years, and they were helpful to us in shipping equipment, even lethal equipment, in and out of out of Afghanistan." [Speech to Goldman Sachs, 2013 IBD CEO Annual Conference, 6/4/13]

Hillary Clinton: "We Would Very Much like to Have a Positive Relationship with Russia and We Would like to See Putin Be Less Defensive toward a Relationship with the United States."

"So we were making progress, and I think Putin has a different view. Certainly he's asserted himself in a way now that is going to take some management on our side, but obviously we would very much like to have a positive relationship with Russia and we would like to see Putin be less defensive toward a relationship with the United States so that we could work together on some issues." [Speech to Goldman Sachs, 2013 IBD CEO Annual Conference, 6/4/13]

Hillary Clinton Called Vladimir Putin "Interesting" but Said He Was Too Powerful Not to Try to Find Common Ground.

"In terms of interesting, Vladimir Putin is always interesting. You're never quite sure what he's going to do or say next, and he's always—he walks around with, you know, a redwood chip on his shoulder defending and promoting, you know, Mother Russia. So he and I have had our interesting moments. He accused me of personally causing all the riots after the contested election two years ago, but he is someone who you have to deal with. You can't, you know, just wish he would go away. He has a huge country and huge potential for causing problems for many people so I always tried to figure out some way to connect with him, what we could talk about that maybe we had some common ground" [Jewish United Fund Of Metropolitan Chicago Vanguard Luncheon, 10/28/13]

Hillary Clinton Said One Time She Visited Putin and Bonded with Him over Protecting the Habitat of Tigers.

"One time, I was visiting with him in his dacha outside of Moscow, and he was going on and on, you know, just listing all of the problems that he thinks are caused by the United States. And I said, 'Well, you know, Mr.'—at that time, he was still prime minister. I said, 'You know, Mr. Prime Minister, we actually have some things in common. We both want to protect wildlife, and I know how committed you are to protecting the tiger.' I mean, all of a sudden, he sat up straight and his eyes got big and he goes, 'You care about the tiger? I said, 'I care about the tiger, I care about the elephant, I care about the rhinoceros, I care about the whale. I mean, yeah, I think we have a duty. You know, it's an obligation that we as human beings have to protect God's creation.' He goes, 'Come with me.' So we go down the stairs, we go down this long hall, we go into this private inner sanctum. All of his, you know, very beefy security guys are there, they all jump up at attention, you know, they punch a code, he goes through a heavily-armed door. And then we're in an inner, inner sanctum with, you know, just this long, wooden table, and then further back, there's a desk and the biggest map of Russia I ever saw. And he starts talking to me about, you know, the habitat of the tigers and the habitat of the seals and the whales. And it was quite something." [Jewish United Fund of Metropolitan Chicago Vanguard Luncheon, 10/28/13]

Chapter 43

SHANGHAI EXPO

Hillary Clinton Looked into the Shanghai Expo after Being Asked about It on Her First Trip as Secretary to China in 2009.

"On my first trip to China in February of 2009, we had a very long agenda on all of the issues that you can imagine, from North Korea to Tibet. And as I was in the midst of the meeting, the Chinese foreign minister said, 'We are so sorry that the United States will not be participating in our international expo in Shanghai in 2010,' the next year. I'd been really well briefed. Nobody had said anything to me about the expo in Shanghai. And you learn in these positions, you know, to look like, oh yes, of course, the expo. (Laughter.) And I said, 'Well, what is it that really concerns you about that?' (Laughter.) And he said, 'Well, the only two countries not building pavilions are Andorra and the United States.' (Laughter.) I said, 'Well, let me look into that.'" [Hillary Clinton Remarks at the World Affairs Council of Oregon, 4/8/14]

Hillary Clinton: "We Have to Have a Pavilion. So We Hustled around and We Got One Built, Finally."

"I raced back to the hotel and started calling people, 'What is the Shanghai expo?' Oh, it was something that the prior administration delegated to a group that is out of money and they didn't really pull together the corporate sponsors and it's too late. I said, it can't be too late. I mean, I keep picking up all of these translated articles from the Chinese press talking about the decline of the United States. We can't not be there, just us and Andorra, for heaven's sakes. (Laughter.) We have to have a pavilion. So we hustled around and we got one built, finally. I actually went back to Shanghai to make sure that it was being built, stood in the rain, an umbrella over my head and talked about how wonderful it was going to be when it actually was finished." [Hillary Clinton Remarks at the World Affairs Council of Oregon, 4/8/14]

Chapter 44

SIMPSON-BOWLES

Clinton: "Simpson-Bowles... Put Forth the Right Framework. Namely, We Have to Restrain Spending, We Have to Have Adequate Revenues, and We Have to Incentivize Growth. It's a Three-Part Formula... and They Reached an Agreement. but What Is Very Hard to Do Is to Then Take That Agreement If You Don't Believe That You're Going to Be Able to Move the Other Side."

SECRETARY CLINTON: Well, this may be borne more out of hope than experience in the last few years. But Simpson-Bowles—and I know you heard from Erskine earlier today—put forth the right framework. Namely, we have to restrain spending, we have to have adequate revenues, and we have to incentivize growth. It's a three-part formula. The specifics can be negotiated depending upon whether we're acting in good faith or not. And what Senator Simpson and Erskine did was to bring Republicans and Democrats alike to the table, and you had the full range of ideological views from I think Tom Coburn to Dick Durbin. And they reached an agreement. But what is very hard to do is to then take that agreement if you don't believe that you're going to be able to move the other side. And where we are now is in this gridlocked dysfunction. So you've got Democrats saying that, you know, you have

176 *Christian Mellor*

to have more revenues; that's the sine qua non of any kind of agreement. You have Republicans saying no, no, no on revenues; you have to cut much more deeply into spending. Well, looks what's happened. We are slowly returning to growth. It's not as much or as fast as many of us would like to see, but, you know, we're certainly better off than our European friends, and we're beginning to, I believe, kind of come out of the long aftermath of the '08 crisis. [Clinton Speech for Morgan Stanley, 4/18/13]

Clinton: "The Simpson-Bowles Framework and the Big Elements of It Were Right... You Have to Restrain Spending, You Have to Have Adequate Revenues, and You Have to Have Growth."

CLINTON: So, you know, the Simpson-Bowles framework and the big elements of it were right. The specifics can be negotiated and argued over. But you got to do all three. You have to restrain spending, you have to have adequate revenues, and you have to have growth. And I think we are smart enough to figure out how to do that. [Clinton Speech for Morgan Stanley, 4/18/13]

Clinton on Bowles-Simpson: "I'm Not Going to Sort of Piecemeal All Their Recommendations, but Their Overall Approach Is Right, Because Here's What They Basically Say. They Say We Need to Constrain Spending, We Need to Have Adequate Revenues, and We've Got to Incentivize Growth."

MR. BOZZUTO: Well, that's a great segway to the next question. We had Alan Simpson of Erskine Bowles here in January speaking to us about the economy. They've now come out with a second set of recommendations. What—putting aside their recommendation, what do you think we need to do as a country to deal with the deficit? SECRETARY CLINTON: Well, both of them are friends. Erskine is a very close friend, and Alan Simpson is someone who you can't help but like. And I really think they're great patriots. I mean, what they've done because they just love this country really is deserving of our respect.

Simpson-Bowles 177

Now, I'm not going to sort of piecemeal all their recommendations, but their overall approach is right, because here's what they basically say. They say we need to constrain spending, we need to have adequate revenues, and we've got to incentivize growth. I mean, that's pretty much the framework for Simpson-Bowles. [Clinton Speech for National Multi-Housing Council, 4/24/13]

Clinton on Budget Politics: "We Need Reasonable, Rational, Moderate Voices on Both Sides of the Aisle... Do We Have to Do Something about Entitlements? Yes. Do We Have to Figure out What We Want to Be as a Nation and Then Pay for It? Yes. Do We Have to Restrain Spending so That We Don't Bankrupt Ourselves and Undermine Our Position at Home and Abroad? Yes."

CLINTON: The devil, as is usually the case, is in the details, because everybody has their own particular idea of what each of those goals mean and the tactics and strategies that we should deploy to get there. Now, Erskine was in the White House, working for my husband, he was Chief of Staff when the budget deal of the late '90s was reached. It was not easy by any means. There was a lot of stray voltage about. You know, we can't compromise, you have to hold your ground, we can't give in, this is sacred, that is sacred. But it was an intensive effort that my husband and Erskine and the team in that administration were engaged in with their congressional counterparts, and they just kept at it, and they just kept sort of burrowing in and making the case and finally reaching an agreement that led to balanced budgets. And, I might add, if we had stayed with the trajectory for the budget that came out of the Clinton Administration, we actually would have paid off the debt. So it wasn't only eliminating, over time, the deficit, but it would have actually paid off the debt. So, I think the—the formula's easy to say, but the politics are very hard. And I guess, you know, Tom, I would say that, in my family, we always say you got to get caught trying, and you have to keep trying. There's too much at stake. The idea that we put the creditworthiness of the gold-plated economy, the U.S.

economy, at risk over the fiscal cliff debate—I was in Hong Kong during that debate in the summer of 2011, and it was embarrassing. It was even a little painful for me because I was speaking to a big Hong Kong business group, and they were multinational executives there, a lot of Chinese were there, both mainland and Hong Kong, and they were just incredulous. They kept saying, now, explain to me, your Congress may let—may say you cannot pay your debts? I mean, explain that to me. And I said, oh, no, that'll never happen. We'll figure it out. We're—you know, we often cause these problems. Like Winston Churchill said, you know, the Americans try everything first before they finally get to the right decision. So, I guess I'm of the school that we will, by necessity, have to get to the right decision. But I think that's where a lot of you come in. Really, we need—we need reasonable, rational, moderate voices on both sides of the aisle to say, you know, we've spent, you know, 230-plus years building up this economy, you know, settling this great country, doing everything we're so proud of as Americans. We're smart enough to figure this out, but it requires compromise on both sides, you know? Nobody in a democracy—it's part of the DNA of a democracy—has all the answers, and so let's just keep at it. Do we have to do something about entitlements? Yes. Do we have to figure out what we want to be as a nation and then pay for it? Yes. Do we have to restrain spending so that we don't bankrupt ourselves and undermine our position at home and abroad? Yes. We all know those things. So, I really think that we have to get back into the business of democracy and listening to each other, working with each other, and quit drawing lines and taking positions that are against compromise of any kind, because, I don't know, maybe I've just lived long enough. I think usually, you know, you try to come to the table and figure out how to make it as close to a win-win as you can, and I think that's what we've got to do, and the whole world is watching us. [Clinton Speech for National Multi-Housing Council, 4/24/13]

Chapter 45

SYRIA

Hillary Clinton Said There Has Not Been the Level of Cooperation and Deportation of the Chemical Weapons out of Syria That We Expected at This Time.

"SECRETARY CLINTON: Well, this is an issue I certainly spent a lot of time working on and worrying about both when I was in the government and in the time since. Taking your last question first the agreement that the Asad regime entered into to disable and remove the chemical weapon stocks was a positive step but it has not been fulfilled. There has not been the level of cooperation and deportation of the chemical precursors and weapon stocks that we had expected by this time. Now, is that because Asad and his government are making it very difficult if not impossible to do that? Is it because in a war, an active conflict like what is happening in Syria it is very difficult to do? It's a hard question to answer but the fact is indisputable, we have not done yet what Asad promised would be done and so we have to stay focused on getting the chemical weapon stocks out of Syria." [02262014 HWA Remarks at UMiami.DOC, p. 18]

180   *Christian Mellor*

Hillary Clinton on Syria: A "Singular Accomplishment" Was Removing the Chemical Weapons out of Syria.

"So the predictions about all of the dangers that could happen have happened. And we never got a chance to try any different approach. However, it is a singular accomplishment to be removing the chemical weapons out of Syria. They are now up to over half of the weapons, the stockpiles, the precursors, being taken out, and they will be destroyed. So that is a positive." [Hillary Clinton Remarks at the World Affairs Council of Oregon, 4/8/14]

Clinton Said She Negotiated Syria Transition Plan to Remove Al-Assad as Outcome Instead of Condition.

"I negotiated an agreement in Geneva last year for a transition plan; and to get the Russians on board we said, you know, we are not going to say that al-Assad has to go as a condition but as an outcome. I mean we really tried to fashion it to get the Russians on board. We thought we had them on board and then that we would go to the Security Council, now, what is called Article 7, no authority to do anything militarily, but to create a framework that could possibly move us forward. And this is obviously my biased view, but the Russians reneged." [Clinton Remarks at Boston Consulting Group, 6/20/13]

Discussing Syria, Clinton Mentioned Boots on the Ground as a Tool to Help Eliminate Chemical and Biological Weapons.

AUDIENCE MEMBER: Secretary Clinton—Madam Secretary, if there was indisputable evidence that the Syrian government used chemical weapons on its people, would you be in favor of armed American intervention in the form of air strikes or boots on the ground? SECRETARY CLINTON: Well, you've asked a very, very difficult question, because we obviously talked about this at great length, and both the United States and Europe, as well as Israel, have said that's a red line. And if there is indisputable evidence, then there is the stated

Syria 181

commitment to take action. What that action is and what would work is extremely difficult to plan and execute. You mentioned air strikes. If you—it depends on who you're trying to strike. If you strike those who are transporting chemical or biological weapons that they have taken from storage depots, you could create an environmental and health catastrophe. If you strike the locations themselves, you have the same problems. When we go in and try to eliminate the danger posed by chemical and biological weapons, it is a very intense, long effort. You have highly trained people who have to handle this material. We've been working—"we" meaning the United States government, along with other contributing nations, have been working in some places for a long period of time. That requires not just boots on the ground, it requires, you know, being able to, in effect, liberate such a depot or such a convoy from those who are currently in charge of it. And then it requires managing the material so it doesn't have disastrous consequences. And then it requires bringing in and protecting the experts long enough that they can take hold of and, in effect, disarm the weaponry. Now, some of it is in storage, it's not prepared at the moment to be immediately used. But we think, and there's a current analysis going on as you're probably aware based on information the Europeans, Israelis and we have, that some of it has been moved, and maybe some in a relatively minor but still very dangerous way has been used. I don't think the analysis is completed on that, and obviously I can't speak to it. So yes, in order to—we have to know which are the most vulnerable sites. There's been a lot of discussion with the Russians. This was something that was very much on my agenda, because they still have channels into the Syrian military. There's a special department within the Syrian military charged with the responsibility of safeguarding chemical and biological stockpiles. The Russians have been communicating with those groups. And all I can tell you is it will have to be stopped if there is evidence that it has been used. It will also have to be stopped if it appears that al-Qaeda's affiliate and/or Hezbollah is moving to take control over it. But that's a lot easier said than done. And given—in a conflict situation like this where you have no idea the loyalties or the mixed interests of those who might be in charge of whatever the sites are. So there's a lot more that could be discussed about this, but it is a very serious problem that our military and our intelligence people have been analyzing and working on for some time. [Clinton Speech for Deutsche Bank, 4/24/13]

On the Initial Syrian Uprising, Hillary Clinton Said Assad Could Have "Bought Them off with Some Cosmetic Changes" That Would Not Have Resulted in the Ongoing Chaos.

"So let's just take a step back and look at the situation that we currently have in Syria. When—before the uprising started in Syria it was clear that you had a minority government running with the Alawites in lead with mostly the other minority groups—Christians, the Druze, some significant Sunni business leaders. But it was clearly a minority that sat on top of a majority. And the uprisings when they began were fairly mild in terms of what they were asking for, and Assad very well could have in my view bought them off with some cosmetic changes that would not have resulted in what we have seen over the now two years and the hundred thousand deaths and the destabilization that is going on in Lebanon, in Jordan, even in Turkey, and the threat throwing to Israel and the kind of pitched battle in Iran well supported by Russia, Saudi, Jordanians and others trying to equip the majority Sunni fighters." [Speech to Goldman Sachs, 2013 IBD CEO Annual Conference, 6/4/13]

Hillary Clinton Said the Russians See Syria as Chechnya and Support "Absolutely Merciless Reactions to Drive down the Opposition to Be Strangled."

"The Russian's view of this is very different. I mean, who conceives Syria as the same way he sees Chechnya? You know, you

Syria 183

have to support toughness and absolute merciless reactions in order to drive the opposition down to be strangled, and you can't give an inch to them and you have to be willing to do what Assad basically has been willing to do." [Speech to Goldman Sachs, 2013 IBD CEO Annual Conference, 6/4/13]

Hillary Clinton Said the Russians Wanted to Provide Assad with Enough Weapons to Maintain Control over Most of the Country and Protect Their Naval Base.

"The Russians' view is that if we provide enough weapons to Assad and if Assad is able to maintain control over most of the country, including the coastal areas where our naval base is, that's fine with us. Because you will have internal fighting still with the Kurds and with the Sunnis on the spectrum of extremism. But if we can keep our base and we can keep Assad in the titular position of running the country, that reflects well on us because we will demonstrate that we are back in the Middle East. Maybe in a ruthless way, but a way that from their perspective, the Russian perspective, Arabs will understand." [Speech to Goldman Sachs, 2013 IBD CEO Annual Conference, 6/4/13]

Hillary Clinton Said Her View Personally Was for the West to Develop Covert Connections with the Syrian Opposition to Gain Insight.

"So the problem for the US and the Europeans has been from the very beginning: What is it you—who is it you are going to try to arm? And you probably read in the papers my view was we should try to find some of the groups that were there that we thought we could build relationships with and develop some covert connections that might then at least give us some insight into what is going on inside Syria." [Speech to Goldman Sachs, 2013 IBD CEO Annual Conference, 6/4/13]

Hillary Clinton Said It Was Fair to Argue "We Don't Know What Will Happen" and Said the Big Problem Was That Iran Was Heavily Invested in Sustaining Assad.

"But the other side of the argument was a very—it was a very good one, which is we don't know what will happen. We can't see down the road. We just need to stay out of it. The problem now is that you've got Iran in heavily. You've got probably at least 50,000 fighters inside working to support, protect and sustain Assad. And like any war, at least the wars that I have followed, the hard guys who are the best fighters move to the forefront." [Speech to Goldman Sachs, 2013 IBD CEO Annual Conference, 6/4/13]

Hillary Clinton Said the Free Syrian Army Was No Match for "These Imported Toughened Iraqi, Jordanian, Libyan, Indonesian, Egyptian, Chechen, Uzbek, Pakistani Fighters That Are Now in There."

"So the free Syrian Army and a lot of the local rebel militias that were made up of pharmacists and business people and attorneys and teachers—they're no match for these imported toughened Iraqi, Jordanian, Libyan, Indonesian, Egyptian, Chechen, Uzbek, Pakistani fighters that are now in there and have learned through more than a decade of very firsthand experience what it takes in terms of ruthlessness and military capacity." [Speech to Goldman Sachs, 2013 IBD CEO Annual Conference, 6/4/13]

Hillary Clinton: "My View Was You Intervene as Covertly as Is Possible for Americans to Intervene. We Used to Be Much Better at This Than We Are Now."

"So we now have what everybody warned we would have, and I am very concerned about the spillover effects. And there is still an argument that goes on inside the administration and inside our friends at NATO and the Europeans. How do intervene—my view was you intervene as covertly as is possible for Americans to intervene. We used to be much better at this than we are now. Now, you know, everybody can't help themselves. They have to go out and tell their friendly reporters and somebody else: Look what we're doing and I want credit for it, and all the rest of it" [Speech to Goldman Sachs, 2013 IBD CEO Annual Conference, 6/4/13]

Hillary Clinton Said One of the Problems with a No Fly Zone Would Be the Need to Take out Syria's Air Defense, and "You're Going to Kill a Lot of Syrians."

"So we're not as good as we used to be, but we still—we can still deliver, and we should have in my view been trying to do that so we would have better insight. But the idea that we would have like a no fly zone—Syria, of course, did have when it started the fourth biggest Army in the world. It had very sophisticated air defense systems. They're getting more sophisticated thanks to Russian imports. To have a no fly zone you have to take out all of the air defense, many of which are located in populated areas. So our missiles, even if they are standoff missiles so we're not putting our pilots at risk—you're going to kill a lot of Syrians. So all of a sudden this intervention that people talk about so glibly becomes an American and NATO involvement where you take a lot of civilians." [Speech to Goldman Sachs, 2013 IBD CEO Annual Conference, 6/4/13]

Hillary Clinton Said Libya Was Simpler Because Their Air Defense Was Not Sophisticated and "There Were Very Few Civilian Casualties."

"In Libya we didn't have that problem. It's a huge place. The air defenses were not that sophisticated and there wasn't very— in fact, there were very few civilian casualties. That wouldn't be the case. And then you add on to it a lot of the air defenses are not only in civilian population centers but near some of their chemical stockpiles. You do not want a missile hitting a chemical stockpile." [Speech to Goldman Sachs, 2013 IBD CEO Annual Conference, 6/4/13]

Hillary Clinton Said the Israelis Carried out Two Raids that Targeted Weapons Convoys in Syria.

"MS. CLINTON: Israel cares a lot about it. Israel, as you know, carried out two raids that were aimed at convoys of weapons and maybe some other stuff, but there was clearly weapons. Part of the tradeoff that the Iranians negotiated with Assad. So I mean, I've described the problem. I haven't given you a solution for it, but I think that the complexity of it speaks to what we're going to be facing in this region, and that leads me to Iran." [Speech to Goldman Sachs, 2013 IBD CEO Annual Conference, 6/4/13]

Hillary Clinton Said the Rejection of Military Strikes to Enforce the Red Line in Syria Was More about Domestic Politics.

"SECRETARY CLINTON: Well, I'm an optimist, so I think the trend line continues to be positive, but I think you have highlighted one of the issues that, you know, concerns me on the—you know, if you look at the—the Syria vote is a bit of a challenging one to draw large conclusions from because it is a wicked problem. There are so many factors at play there. But the underlying rejection of a military strike to enforce the red line on chemical weapons spoke more about, you know, the country's preoccupation with our own domestic situation, the feeling that we need to get our own house in order, that we need to get that economy that everybody here is so deeply involved in producing more, getting back to growth, dealing with the unemployment figures that are still unacceptably high in too many places." [Goldman Sachs Builders and Innovators Summit, 10/29/13]

Syria

Hillary Clinton Said "You Can't Squander Your Reputation and Your Leadership Capital. You Have to Do What You Say You're Going to Do."

"So it was both a rejection of any military action in the Middle East right now and a conclusion that, you know, people of considerable analytical understanding of the region could also reach that, you know, you—we're in—we're in a time in Syria where they're not finished killing each other, where it's very difficult for anybody to predict a good outcome and maybe you just have to wait and watch it. But on the other side of it, you can't squander your reputation and your leadership capital. You have to do what you say you're going to do. You have to be smart about executing on your strategies. And you've got to be careful not to send the wrong message to others, such as Iran." [Goldman Sachs Builders and Innovators Summit, 10/29/13]

Hillary Clinton Said Jordan Was Threatened Because "They Can't Possibly Vet All Those Refugees so They Don't Know If, You Know, Jihadists Are Coming in along with Legitimate Refugees."

"So I think you're right to have gone to the places that you visited because there's a discussion going on now across the region to try to see where there might be common ground to deal with the threat posed by extremism and particularly with Syria which has everyone quite worried, Jordan because it's on their border and they have hundreds of thousands of refugees and they can't possibly vet all those refugees so they don't know if, you know, jihadists are coming in along with legitimate refugees. Turkey for the same reason." [Jewish United Fund of Metropolitan Chicago Vanguard Luncheon, 10/28/13]

Hillary Clinton Said Some Advice in Syria to "Let Them Kill Themselves until They Get Exhausted, and Then We'll Figure out How to Deal with What the Remnants Are."

"One way is a very hands off, step back, we don't have a dog in this hunt, let them kill themselves until they get exhausted, and then we'll figure out how to deal with what the remnants are. That's a position held by people who believe that there is no way, not just for the United States but others, to stop the killing before the people doing the killing and the return killing are tired of killing each other. So it's a very hands-off approach." [2014 Jewish United Fund Advance & Major Gifts Dinner, 10/28/13]

Hillary Clinton Called the Removal of Syria's Chemical Weapons a "Net Positive."

"So that happens to be moving forward, which in and of itself is a positive. It doesn't stop the civil war. It doesn't stop the continued abuses and murders and everything that goes with it, but it is a net positive for the world and our national interest if we can disable Syria's large chemical stockpiles, begin to actually ship it out of the country, get it away from terrorist networks and others." [2014 Jewish United Fund Advance & Major Gifts Dinner, 10/28/13]

Hillary Clinton Said She Favored "More Robust, Covert Action" in Syria but Said Things Have Been "Complicated by the Fact That the Saudis and Others Are Shipping Large Amounts of Weapons— and Pretty Indiscriminately."

"Now, there is another group, which basically argued we do have a national interest in this because refugee flows, jihadist recruitment, giving of large parts of Syria over to uncontrollable groups that threaten Israel, Jordan and others, through conventional means is very much against our interests, and the debate has been can you really influence

Syria 189

that? Some of us thought, perhaps, we could, with a more robust, covert action trying to vet, identify, train and arm cadres of rebels that would at least have the firepower to be able to protect themselves against both Assad and the Al-Qaeda related jihadist groups that have, unfortunately, been attracted to Syria. That's been complicated by the fact that the Saudis and others are shipping large amounts of weapons— and pretty indiscriminately—not at all targeted toward the people that we think would be the more moderate, least likely, to cause problems in the future, but this is another one of those very tough analytical problems." [2014 Jewish United Fund Advance & Major Gifts Dinner, 10/28/13]

Hillary Clinton Said the US Had "Potential National Interests" in Syria.

"It depends upon how you define national interest. We certainly do with chemical weapons. We certainly would if Syria became even, in part, like the FATA between Pakistan and Afghanistan, a training ground for extremists, a launching pad for attacks on Turkey, Jordan, the non-tetarian elements in Lebanon and, eventually, even in Israel. So that would certainly be a national interest and how we would cope with that, if that were to come to pass. So it's—it is a particularly tough issue because I think we have national interests right now. I think we have potential future national interests but trying to figure out the best way for us to pursue those interests has been quite challenging." [2014 Jewish United Fund Advance & Major Gifts Dinner, 10/28/13]

Hillary Clinton: "I Was among the President's Advisors Who Favored a More Robust, Covert Effort to Try to Figure out Who, If Anybody, We Could Know More about and Possibly Partner With."

"MS. HILLARY CLINTON: Well, that's where we are right now. I mean I was among the President's advisors who favored a more robust, covert effort to try to figure out who, if anybody, we could know more about and possibly partner with, but for all kinds of reasons that didn't come to pass. So the chemical weapons piece is something that we need to carry through on, and getting the chemical weapons out of there while we actually have an Assad regime to work with is a very important development. It helps remove one of the fears and, frankly, one of the—one of the issues on our checklist as to what would happen with all of these chemical weapons that may make whatever we do next somewhat more understandable." [2014 Jewish United Fund Advance & Major Gifts Dinner, 10/28/13]

Chapter 46

TAXES

CORPORATE TAXES

Hillary Clinton Said We Have to Rationalize Our Tax System Because She Doesn't Want to See Biotech and Pharma Companies Moving out of the Country.

"The tax issue is something else. Clearly, I believe we've got to rationalize our tax system, because I don't want to see biotech companies or pharma companies moving out of our country simply because of some kind of tax -- perceived tax disadvantage and potential tax advantage somewhere else. (Applause.)" [06252014 HWA Remarks at BIO (San Diego, CA).docx, p. 6]

Hillary Clinton on Tax on Foreign Earnings: "I Would like to Figure out Ways of Getting It Back and Figuring out Some Creative Ways."

HILLARY CLINTON: "Well, I would like to find a way to repatriate the overseas earnings and I've read a really interesting proposal. I haven't vetted it, so I don't know all the details of it. But, John Chambers and others, of big companies like you're saying, they

192   *Christian Mellor*

basically have said they would be willing to invest a percentage of their repatriated profits in an infrastructure bank that would be doing what we need to be doing, increasing our infrastructure, everything from repairing airports and ports, and broadband access being increased dramatically and a long list of what we're not doing. And I thought that was a really intriguing idea, because it doesn't do us – it doesn't do our economy any good to have this money parked somewhere else in the world and it's not really being put to use there either. So I would like to figure out ways of getting it back and figuring out some creative ways." [Hillary Clinton Remarks at Nexenta, 8/28/14]

In Fielding Question about US Corporate Tax Reform, Hillary Clinton Mentioned Her Frequent Meetings with Corporate Executives and "Groups All across the Private Sector."

HILLARY CLINTON: "This time around, a number of business leaders have been talking to my husband and me about an idea that would allow the repatriation of the couple trillion dollars that are out there. And you would get a lower rate -- a really low rate -- if you were willing to invest a percentage in an infrastructure bank. Because it's so interesting to me, I meet with lots of corporate executives, I talk to groups from all across the private sector, and they all complain about our infrastructure. Complain about our bad rail systems, and particularly with the increased burden that the rails are carrying because of oil and gas tankers. They complain about our airports, they complain about our ports, they complain about our roads." [Hillary Clinton Remarks at Council of Insurance Agents and Brokers, 10/13/14]

Clinton Said Lowering the Corporate Tax Rate Could "Be on the Table and to Be Looked at as Part of a Broader Package" to Make America More Competitive.

"JACK LEWIN: Very good. Thank you. Some of the questions came from this audience. We had a whole lot of them. But a parallel to this question was one about the corporate tax rate. The U.S. corporate

Taxes 193

tax rate is higher than most of our developed nation colleagues. And so I think without kind of a real sincere just what if we looked at that one area as a means of improving our international ability to compete in the global economy? Is that something, have you thought about that at all? SEC. HILLARY CLINTON: Well, you know, I think that there are a number of reforms that we should consider to make ourselves more competitive. That certainly could be on the table and to be looked at as part of a broader package, because if all you do is lower the rates and you don't have some path forward as to what you're trying to achieve and what the loss revenues might mean for pick your favorite subject, basic science or whatever it might be. Then there's a price to pay. You have to be prepared to pay that price." [Remarks to Cardiovascular Research Foundation, 9/15/14]

Hillary Clinton Said "the Corporate Tax Code Is, You Know, an Impediment and Kind of a Dinosaur Waiting to Be Changed."

"MODERATOR KRUEGER: Speaking about remaining competitive to do business on a global basis, our tax code; there may be one or two humans who can understand it, I'm not sure anymore. There seems—you know, we have the highest corporate tax rate in the world. In one sense we've made this country the most non-competitive place to be headquartered and do business directly. There seems to be a growing consensus we need tax reform. There seems to be two camps. One, let's nibble around the edges, let's adjust a few provisions. The other camp seems to be, trash it, go big, go bold, and go simple. Do you have any inclinations, one way or the other? SECRETARY CLINTON: Well, I think we should go smart. I mean, I think that part of our challenge is to do what we have to do, which is to take a hard look at our tax code and connect it to what our national goals are, you know, what is it we need to be collecting taxes to do, and what is it we need to make it, in essence, so we become more competitive in the future, and that requires the kind of thoughtful discussion that we haven't had enough of in recent years. I think there are very good arguments that need to be aired. I agree with you, the corporate tax code is, you know, an impediment and kind of a dinosaur waiting to be changed." [Hillary Clinton remarks to ECGR Grand Rapids, 6/17/13]

SIMPLIFYING TAX CODE

Clinton: "We Can Save Money and Become More Competitive with a Simpler Tax Code Related to What We Are Trying to Achieve."

"How it fits into an overall tax code is something that has to be given close consideration, but I believe we can save money and become more competitive with a simpler tax code related to what we are trying to achieve." [Hillary Clinton remarks to ECGR Grand Rapids, 6/17/13]

Chapter 47

TECHNOLOGY/NEW ECONOMY

Hillary Clinton Said Technological Change "Can Empower Corporations That Are Trying to Help Build a Middle Class and Spread Prosperity."

"We see the important role of economies even more than militaries in helping to shape foreign affairs, and the political and technological changes are also empowering non-state actors. That is both good and bad because they can empower activists who are fighting corruption or are fighting for environmental sustainability or fighting for education for girls. They can empower corporations that are trying to help build a middle class and spread prosperity. And they can also empower terrorist networks and criminal cartels." [Remarks at London Drug Toronto, 11/4/13]

Chapter 48

TERRORISM

Hillary Clinton: Terrorism "Not a Threat to Us as a Nation," but Remains "a Real Threat."

"But make no mistake, as the recent travel alert underscores, we still face terrorism. It's not a threat to us as a nation. It is not going to endanger our economy or our society, but it is a real threat. It is a danger to our citizens here at home, and as we tragically saw in Boston, and to those living, working, and traveling abroad." [Hillary Clinton remarks to Global Business Travelers Association, 8/7/13]

Clinton: "We Used to Have a Kind of Top Ten List of Targets, and When We'd Kill One, We'd Move the Next Most Important Guy into the Line-Up."

CLINTON: Secondly, we did really, both in the Bush Administration and in the Obama Administration, go right at core Al Qaeda. You know, we have, you know, killed and captured so many of their leaders. We used to have a kind of top ten list of targets, and when we'd kill one, we'd move the next most important guy into the line-up. So, we really took out their command and control, and, of course, getting bin Laden was an essential, necessary act of our own self-

198 *Christian Mellor*

defense because even in that compound in Abbottabad, he was still communicating, he was still plotting, he was still trying to inspire more attacks against us. [Clinton Speech for National Multi-Housing Council, 4/24/13]

Hillary Clinton Said "There Are People like" Nuclear Terrorists from James Bonds Movies.

"And you know, it is like these terrible plots in James Bond movies where you have got some really creepy guy sitting around saying, I want to get a hold of some nuclear material, and I can bring the west to their knees and they will have to give me a hundred billion dollars in my private account. Well, unfortunately, there are people like that. And we saw what happened with the Pakistani scientist, Mr. Khan, who basically proliferated nuclear knowledge to as many countries as he could. He thought that was part of his religious mission to give the bomb to as many Muslim countries as he possibly could reach." [Remarks at London Drug Toronto, 11/4/13]

Chapter 49

Unpaid Internships

Hillary Clinton Said Businesses Have Taken Advantage of Unpaid Internships to That Extent That It Prevents Young People to Move to Paid Employment.

"Too often when training is available or when education is consumed, it's for jobs that don't actually exist or for industries that are shrinking. There are not enough opportunities for young people to get paid for on-the-job experience outside of the classroom, which is what businesses look for. But also, let's be honest, businesses have taken advantage of unpaid internships to an extent that it is blocking the opportunities for young people to move on into paid employment. So, yes, internships are great and provide a valuable experience, but that is not a job. And more businesses need to move their so-called interns to employees. And we have to do more to seek out those people with workforce training programs and employers looking to hire." [03052014 HWA Remarks at UCLA.doc, p. 13]

Chapter 50

WALL STREET

BLAME FOR FINANCIAL CRISIS

Clinton Said That the Blame Placed on the United States Banking System for the Crisis "Could Have Been Avoided in Terms of Both Misunderstanding and Really Politicizing What Happened."

"That was one of the reasons that I started traveling in February of '09, so people could, you know, literally yell at me for the United States and our banking system causing this everywhere. Now, that's an oversimplification we know, but it was the conventional wisdom. And I think that there's a lot that could have been avoided in terms of both misunderstanding and really politicizing what happened with greater transparency, with greater openness on all sides, you know, what happened, how did it happen, how do we prevent it from happening? You guys help us figure it out and let's make sure that we do it right this time. And I think that everybody was desperately trying to fend off the worst effects institutionally, governmentally, and there just wasn't that opportunity to try to sort this out, and that came later." [Goldman Sachs AIMS Alternative Investments Symposium, 10/24/13]

FUTURES MARKETS

Clinton Joked It's "Risky" for Her to Speak to a Group Committed to Futures Markets Given Her Past Whitewater Scandal.

"Now, it's always a little bit risky for me to come speak to a group that is committed to the futures markets because—there's a few knowing laughs—many years ago, I actually traded in the futures markets. I mean, this was so long ago, it was before computers were invented, I think. And I worked with a group of like-minded friends and associates who traded in pork bellies and cotton and other such things, and I did pretty well. I invested about a thousand dollars and traded up to about a hundred thousand. And then my daughter was born, and I just didn't think I had enough time or mental space to figure out anything having to do with trading other than trading time with my daughter for time with the rest of my life. So I got out, and I thought that would be the end of it." [Remarks to CME Group, 11/18/13]

Clinton Noted That Republican Leo Melamed, in the Audience, Reviewed Her and President Clinton's Trades during Whitewater and "Concluded I Hadn't Done Anything Wrong."

"Fast forward to the '90s. My husband is president, and all of a sudden everything we did, whether we made money or lost money, was considered fodder for political opposition and media scrutiny. So people were saying, "How could you make that much money in the futures market back in the late '70s?" And we were -- we'd been audited. It wasn't like we were hiding anything, but, no, they wanted an independent assessment. So we said, "Well, who can we get that is totally independent and nobody will say he's, you know, in cahoots with Bill and me?" And so somebody said, "Well, Leo Melamed. Have him take a look at your trades. He's a Republican. He doesn't -- has never supported your husband. But if you ask him to do it, he will, in characteristic fashion, say whatever he finds." I thought, "Well, okay."

Wall Street 203

And sure enough, that's what Leo, who's here today, did. He looked at all my little pathetic trades and concluded I hadn't done anything wrong, said it was a tempest in a teapot. That took all of the air out of the balloons, but I've been a little nervous about coming around futures markets ever since." [Remarks to CME Group, 11/18/13]

GOALS OF WALL STREET

Clinton Said of Wall Street, "You Have to Keep Looking over the Horizon to Make Choices That Are Not Only Going to Benefit You But...The Larger Economy."

"I was struck by an op-ed that Terry had in the *Wall Street Journal* about two months ago. It was titled "Wall Street is Losing the Best and the Brightest," but it was really about the disconnect that is growing between our financial markets and our economy between, as Terry said, Wall Street and Main Street. Now, one thing that came through to me loudly and clearly as Secretary of State for four years is that you have to keep looking to the future. That's what you do, and you do it extremely well. You have to keep looking over the horizon to make choices that are going to not only benefit you but your institutions and, I would hope, the larger economy." [Remarks to CME Group, 11/18/13]

PRAISING WALL STREET

At a Goldman Summit, Hillary Clinton Said "Many of You in This Room Are Masters of the Trend Lines. You See over the Horizon, You Think about Products That Nobody Has Invented, and You Go about the Business of Trying to Do That."

"And, you know, let me just briefly say that one of the ways I look at domestic as well as international issues is by trying to focus not just on the headlines, although those are insistent and demand your attention, but to keep an eye on the trend lines. And many of you in this room are masters of the trend lines. You see over the horizon, you think about products that nobody has invented, and you go about the business of trying to do that." [Goldman Sachs Builders and Innovators Summit, 10/29/13]

Hillary Clinton Praised "Continuing Movements towards Open Markets" and "toward the Development of a Middle Class That Can Buy the Products."

"But the trend lines are both positive and troubling. There is a still continuing movement toward open markets, toward greater innovation, toward the development of a middle class that can buy the products. As Lloyd was talking in his intro about the work that you do creating products and then making sure there's markets by fostering the kind of inclusive prosperity that includes consumers is a positive trend in many parts of the world now. Democracy is holding its own, so people are still largely living under governments of their own choosing. The possibilities of technology increasing lifespan and access to education and so many other benefits that will redound to not only the advantage of the individual but larger society." [Goldman Sachs Builders and Innovators Summit, 10/29/13]

Clinton Thanked Deutsche Bank for Their Work on Affordable Housing, Economic Development, Clean Energy, Clean Water, Their Work for CGI and Other Good Works.

CLINTON: I want to begin by recognizing the many contributions that everyone here at Deutsche Bank has made to our communities and our world. We'll get into the serious stuff and the story telling later on in the Q&A. But I just want to pause for a very short recognition of the work that the Bank has done in New York City on affordable housing, on economic development, on education and the arts; the contributions to global efforts on clean energy, clean water and helping to build

Wall Street

205

markets in developing countries for clean, safe and affordable cook stoves that could literally save millions of lives and also diminish the contribution of climate forcers like carbon and black soot and methane. But perhaps most notable has been your ongoing support for microloans for both men and women, but mostly women, because they are the primary borrowers under microloan programs: women with no access to credit, no financial tools, few opportunities for employment or advancement, but, you know, with ideas, with energy and with ambition. And research from the World Bank shows what you obviously know, which is that when women participate in the economy, the benefits ripple across communities and societies. And since 1997 Deutsche Bank has dedicated more than $215 million in empowering 2.8 million emerging entrepreneurs in 50 countries. And I also want to thank you for the announcement at last September's meeting of the Clinton Global Initiative in New York that the bank launched a new $50 million fund to support this kind of socially-responsible impact investing. I greatly appreciate all of your efforts, and microfinance is something I've worked on for nearly 30 years. [Clinton Speech for Deutsche Bank, 4/24/13]

Clinton Thanked Morgan Stanley for "Lending" Her Tom Nides.

"And I want to say to James and everyone at Morgan Stanley, thank you for lending me Tom Nides for the past two years. There was a bit of a culture shock at first. When I sent him to Baghdad and Kabul and other such places, he had to spend the night in containers that served as the housing for visiting diplomats, even deputy secretaries. You should have seen his face when he learned there were no stock options at the State Department. But he soon not only settled in very nicely, he became positively enthusiastic when I told him we did have our own plane. So Tom, once again, I'm in your most capable hands." [Clinton Speech for Morgan Stanley, 4/18/13]

206   *Christian Mellor*

Clinton Joked Tom Nides Went through Culture Shock When He Realized the Housing Conditions for Visiting Diplomats in Baghdad and Kabul and That There Were No Stock Options.

"And I want to say to James and everyone at Morgan Stanley, thank you for lending me Tom Nides for the past two years. There was a bit of a culture shock at first. When I sent him to Baghdad and Kabul and other such places, he had to spend the night in containers that served as the housing for visiting diplomats, even deputy secretaries. You should have seen his face when he learned there were no stock options at the State Department. But he soon not only settled in very nicely, he became positively enthusiastic when I told him we did have our own plane. So Tom, once again, I'm in your most capable hands." [Clinton Speech for Morgan Stanley, 4/18/13]

Tom Nides Thanked Clinton for Making Morgan Stanley Her First Business Audience after Leaving State.

"Well, Madam Secretary, thank you. I don't think the stock options were [inaudible] but the container was. And there is no Four Seasons in Baghdad, I assure you. Let me just -- first of all, thank you for doing this. As you all know, this is one of the Secretary's first business groups that she has spoken to since she's left the State Department, so we're honored that you would choose Morgan Stanley, and more importantly I'm honored that you'd choose our clients to come and spend a few minutes with." [Clinton Speech for Morgan Stanley, 4/18/13]

Clinton: "I Greatly Appreciate When Companies, like Morgan Stanley, Do Work in Communities Here and around the World That Makes a Difference."

"But fundamentally, we have a system that has survived and flourished for so long because we recognize that beyond the contest, the competition, the moment, there are larger values and stakes that we have to keep our eyes on. I think businesses thrive when communities and

Wall Street 207

countries thrive. And I greatly appreciate when companies, like Morgan Stanley, do work in communities here and around the world that makes a difference." [Clinton Speech for Morgan Stanley, 4/18/13]

Clinton Praised Fidelity for Contributing in Communities across America.

"I also know that Fidelity makes important contributions in many communities across America where you do business, and I particularly want to applaud your efforts to help low-income and at-risk students complete middle school and move on to high school with the strongest possible preparation. People don't realize that many dropouts happen as early as ninth grade, and Fidelity got that and is intervening at this crucial time in young people's lives." [Remarks to Fidelity, 4/30/13]

Clinton Said Ameriprise Helped Families "Live the American Dream."

In her remarks at Ameriprise, Hillary Clinton said, "So I thank you. I thank you for the work you do across our country. You contribute to Americans' financial success and security in so many ways. You help families, literally, live the American dream. And I would just ask you to think about what more we could do together. Putting aside partisan differences and trying to get back to good, old-fashioned decision-making based on the best evidence we can get. And realizing that we're all in this together. That how we solve our problems at home will determine the strength of our leadership abroad as well as the strength of our economy. I always tell people, and as I traveled, there were lots of wrinkled brows as Asians in particular would say to me, 'What does it mean that you have people who want to default on the American debt?' And I would say, 'Oh, that won't happen.' And then I'd kind of cross my fingers and hold my breath." [Hillary Clinton's Remarks at Ameriprise, 7/26/14]

DODD-FRANK

Clinton Said Dodd-Frank Was Something That Needed to Pass "for Political Reasons."

"And with political people, again, I would say the same thing, you know, there was a lot of complaining about Dodd-Frank, but there was also a need to do something because for political reasons, if you were an elected member of Congress and people in your constituency were losing jobs and shutting businesses and everybody in the press is saying it's all the fault of Wall Street, you can't sit idly by and do nothing, but what you do is really important. And I think the jury is still out on that because it was very difficult to sort of sort through it all." [Goldman Sachs AIMS Alternative Investments Symposium, 10/24/13]

REGULATORS FROM WALL STREET

Clinton Said Financial Reform "Really Has to Come from the Industry Itself."

"Remember what Teddy Roosevelt did. Yes, he took on what he saw as the excesses in the economy, but he also stood against the excesses in politics. He didn't want to unleash a lot of nationalist, populistic reaction. He wanted to try to figure out how to get back into that balance that has served America so well over our entire nationhood. Today, there's more that can and should be done that really has to come from the industry itself, and how we can strengthen our economy, create more jobs at a time where that's increasingly challenging, to get back to Teddy Roosevelt's square deal. And I really believe that our country and all of you are up to that job." [Clinton Remarks to Deutsche Bank, 10/7/14]

Wall Street 209

Speaking about the Importance of Proper Regulation, Clinton Said "the People That Know the Industry Better Than Anybody Are the People Who Work in the Industry."

"I mean, it's still happening, as you know. People are looking back and trying to, you know, get compensation for bad mortgages and all the rest of it in some of the agreements that are being reached. There's nothing magic about regulations, too much is bad, too little is bad. How do you get to the golden key, how do we figure out what works? And the people that know the industry better than anybody are the people who work in the industry. And I think there has to be a recognition that, you know, there's so much at stake now, I mean, the business has changed so much and decisions are made so quickly, in nano seconds basically. We spend trillions of dollars to travel around the world, but it's in everybody's interest that we have a better framework, and not just for the United States but for the entire world, in which to operate and trade." [Goldman Sachs AIMS Alternative Investments Symposium, 10/24/13]

REPRESENTING WALL STREET

Hillary Clinton Said That after the 9/11 Attacks, She Told President Bush, "We Need $20 Billion. We've Got to Quickly Get the Stock Market Up, We've Got to Quickly Start To... Rebuild Lower Manhattan."

In her remarks at Ameriprise, Hillary Clinton said, "I'll tell you a quick story about President George W. Bush. So we're attacked in 9/11. I go with my colleague, Chuck Schumer, to New York to meet with Governor Pataki, Mayor Giuliani, and other officials, and to go see the horror that had been inflicted on us. The next day, we're in the Oval Office. And we had done some back-of-the-envelope calculations. And we asked President Bush—we were in the Oval Office with the two

210   *Christian Mellor*

senators from Virginia because of the attack on the Pentagon, and Schumer and me. And President Bush said, 'What do I need to do?' And I said, 'We need $20 billion. We've got to quickly get the stock market up, we've got to quickly start spending money in order to rebuild lower Manhattan.' 'Done.' He said, 'You got it.'" [Hillary Clinton's Remarks at Ameriprise, 7/26/14]

Clinton: When I Was a Senator, "a Lot of My Support Came from Those Working in Finance, but That Didn't Stop Me from Calling for Closing the Carried Interest Loophole."

In her remarks at Ameriprise, Hillary Clinton said, "When I was a senator from New York, I represented and worked with so many talented and principled people. And a lot of my support came from those working in finance, but that didn't stop me from calling for closing the carried interest loophole, addressing skyrocketing CEO pay, or today, calling for an end to so-called inversion. Because I saw every day how important a well-functioning financial system is to our economy and to people's wellbeing. That's why I raised early warnings about the subprime mortgage market and called for regulating derivatives and other complex financial products that hardly anybody could explain." [Hillary Clinton's Remarks at Ameriprise, 7/26/14]

Clinton: As Senator, "I Represented and Worked with" so Many on Wall Street and "Did All I Could to Make Sure They Continued to Prosper" but Still Called for Closing Carried Interest Loophole.

In remarks at Robbins, Gellar, Rudman & Dowd in San Diego, Hillary Clinton said, "When I was a Senator from New York, I represented and worked with so many talented principled people who made their living in finance. But even thought I represented them and did all I could to make sure they continued to prosper, I called for closing the carried interest loophole and addressing skyrocketing CEO pay. I also was calling in '06, '07 for doing something about the

Wall Street 211

mortgage crisis, because I saw every day from Wall Street literally to main streets across New York how a well-functioning financial system is essential. So when I raised early warnings about early warnings about subprime mortgages and called for regulating derivatives and over complex financial products, I didn't get some big arguments, because people sort of said, no, that makes sense. But boy, have we had fights about it ever since." [Hillary Clinton's Remarks at Robbins Geller Rudman & Dowd in San Diego, 9/04/14]

Clinton on Wall Street: "I Had Great Relations and Worked so Close Together after 9/11 to Rebuild Downtown, and a Lot of Respect for the Work You Do and the People Who Do It."

"Now, without going over how we got to where we are right now, what would be your advice to the Wall Street community and the big banks as to the way forward with those two important decisions? SECRETARY CLINTON: Well, I represented all of you for eight years. I had great relations and worked so close together after 9/11 to rebuild downtown, and a lot of respect for the work you do and the people who do it, but I do -- I think that when we talk about the regulators and the politicians, the economic consequences of bad decisions back in '08, you know, were devastating, and they had repercussions throughout the world." [Goldman Sachs AIMS Alternative Investments Symposium, 10/24/13]

Goldman Sachs' Representative Thanked Clinton for Her Courage in Continuing to Associate Herself with Wall Street after Crisis.

"MR. O'NEILL: By the way, we really did appreciate when you were the senator from New York and your continued involvement in the issues (inaudible) to be courageous in some respects to associated with Wall Street and this environment. Thank you very much. SECRETARY CLINTON: Well, I don't feel particularly courageous. I mean, if we're going to be an effective, efficient economy, we need to have all part of that engine running well, and that includes Wall Street and Main Street." [Goldman Sachs AIMS Alternative Investments Symposium, 10/24/13]

Chapter 51

WAL-MART

Clinton Recalled Serving on Wal-Mart Board Because Sam Walton Couldn't Think of Anyone Else.

"And, you know, I've served on three public boards. And the first board I ever served on was Walmart. And I had gotten to know Sam Walton because I worked with him on education reform in Arkansas, and one day out of the blue he calls me up. He goes, Hillary Clinton, my wife and my daughter think we need a woman on the board, and I can't think of anybody else. I said, well, that's really flattering, but— but, you know, I think that we've made some progress but not enough progress, and so people need to work on ending those discriminatory thought patterns and stereotyping." [Remarks at Beaumont Society Dinner, 11/6/13]

Clinton Discussed Being on Board of Wal-Mart and Convincing Sam Walton to Raise Corporate Taxes to Pay for Education.

"I was on the board of Wal-Mart back in the late 1980s, and I had done some work on education reform, and I had actually convinced the leading businessmen in Arkansas to agree to raise the corporate income tax to pay for educational improvement. And Sam Walton kept shaking

214 *Christian Mellor*

his head saying, I don't understand how you convinced me to do that. And I said, well, because you became convinced that you need an educated workforce, you need more people in the middle class to buy more of your goods." [International Leaders' Series, Palais des Congrès de Montréal, 3/18/14]

Clinton Discussed Wal-Mart Board Meeting Where She Supported Environmentally Conscious Stores and She Started an Environment Subcommittee.

"So he calls me up one day and he goes, Hillary Clinton, my wife and daughter think we need a woman on the board and we can't think of anybody else besides you. I said, well, you have a way with words, Sam. That's really flattering. But, sure, I'll be on the board of Wal-Mart. And we would go to the board meeting. I was the only woman at the time. And what was such genius about Sam Walton is that he started every board meeting by going around to the outside directors and say, tell me something I don't know. What do you see happening in the world that I don't see happening in the world. And I remember one of those meetings saying, well, I think people are starting to get concerned about the environment. And I think we should do a better job in this company in trying to figure out how to have more energy efficient stores, how to deliver goods more efficiently with less use of fossil fuels as possible, and so I chaired the first little environment subcommittee. And where did I get that idea? I got it from my daughter, who came home from school because in school they'd been talking about the environment. And I listened and then I brought it to another setting. So I think there's evidence that having women in those positions makes a difference." [International Leaders' Series, Palais des Congrès de Montréal, 3/18/14]

Clinton Said Sam Walton Was "a Great Patriot."

"Well, what I was saying in my opening remarks is, you know, it really made a big impression on me that despite your partisan

Wal-Mart

differences or your political ambitions or whatever you think of about how our democracy does or doesn't work, we're all on the American team. And Sam Walton was a cheerleader for Walmart but also a great patriot, because he knew that he was able to build this company in this country, and it might not, if ever, have been possible anywhere else." [Hillary Clinton remarks at Sanford Bernstein, 5/29/13]

Hillary Clinton Talked about Working with Wal-Mart and Other Leading Companies to Reform Arkansas' Education System.

"MR. ZLOTNIKOV: Unfortunately we're running out of time, so I'll ask one last question, and you obviously devoted your life to public service, but you also served on some corporate boards. As you reflect between the sort of two entities, what are the most stark differences in how decisions get made between corporations and governments? SECRETARY CLINTON: Well, I did serve on corporate boards back in the '80s. Probably the experience I learned the most from was Walmart. I had worked, when Bill was governor of Arkansas, to help reform the education system in Arkansas, which back in the early '80s was afflicted by all kinds of problems, including the second lowest paid teachers in the country. And I came up with some specific recommendations that Bill and I then took around to the business leadership in Arkansas, Don Tysen and Witt Stephens of Stephens, Inc., and others and, of course, Sam Walton, and we had this rather interesting and somewhat challenging idea that we needed to pay teachers more in Arkansas. So we'd have a small increase in the sales tax and a small increase in the corporate tax. So I met with Sam Walton and I kind of laid that all out for him and told him why we needed to do it. And he said, well, you know, that makes sense. You've got a good plan. I'll see what I can do. And he actually supported, if you can imagine, a small increase in the corporate tax that would go into education in Arkansas. That was in 1983 and '84." [Hillary Clinton remarks at Sanford Bernstein, 5/29/13]

216 *Christian Mellor*

Hillary Clinton Recounted Sam Walton Asking Her to Join the Board of Wal-Mart.

"About four years later, he called me up one day, said to me, Hillary Clinton, my wife and my daughter say we need a woman on the board and I can't think of anybody else but you. So what'd ya say? I say, well, you know, boy, Sam, that's quite a flattering request. I said, sure, why not, right. So I joined the Walmart board really at the jumping-off point of it becoming not just a national and North American company, but an international company. And what I found, at least the way Sam Walton ran a board, was that it was very much an interactive experience. He would start every board meeting by looking at all the outside directors and saying, okay, tell me something I don't know, tell me something you think is going on in the world, tell me something that is affecting your business or your perspective. And we would spend about an hour, and it would be, well, you know, here's what I think is happening politically or here's what I see as an opportunity or I'm worried about X, Y or Z. He was always, always curious. He was always in a learning mode." [Hillary Clinton remarks at Sanford Bernstein, 5/29/13]

Hillary Clinton Praised Sam Walton as "One of the First American Business Executives to Really Embrace Technology."

"You know, he used to fly his little airplane around driving the FAA crazy. He would land on dirt roads and parking lots, and he would go into a K-Mart and walk up and down the aisles and pigeonhole customers and employees and say, what do you like about working here? What do you like about what you'd buy here? And then he'd go back and he'd say, I learned something over at the K-Mart in the next county, and I want us to try that. He was one of the first American business executives to really embrace technology, and that's a kind of untold story, but he began building up Walmart's technological foundation in the '80s and was prepared with, you know, all of the, you know, the slogans we now do, you know, just in time inventory or whatever it might be before a lot of competitors or even businesses in other sectors." [Hillary Clinton remarks at Sanford Bernstein, 5/29/13]

Clinton Praised Sam Walton, and Said Her Service on the Wal-Mart Board Was the "Most Intriguing" of the Three Public Boards She Served On.

"I ended up serving on three public boards in the next couple of years, and probably the service on the Walmart board was the most intriguing. It was at a time when the company was rapidly expanding and utilizing technology in a way that a lot of other companies, not just retail companies, had not yet pioneered. So I could see for myself what this, you know, transition looked like and how somebody who had started as a small town merchant was transforming this company based in Bentonville, Arkansas to be the, you know, global giant that it is today. He knew how to make decisions, but he also knew how to gather information, and he was a just rabid listener wanting to know what you knew, what you thought was going on in order to make the right decision." [Accenture Women's Leadership Forum, 10/24/13]

Hillary Clinton Talked about Working on Education Reform in Arkansas with Sam Walton, Tyson Foods, "the Oil and Gas Firms," and "the Banks."

"Let me close with two people whose lives and experiences were very different, but who both helped me understand this ethic of shared responsibility, my father and Sam Walton... So when I moved to Arkansas, Sam was already a fixture in the state's business community, and I got to know him and his wonderful family, and Arkansas' education system was in very serious disrepair. The teachers were paid very poorly. Only in the 1980 census about ten percent of the entire state population graduated from college. There was a lot of work to be done. And my husband was governor, and he asked me to work on helping to improve education. And I went to see Sam and talked to him about this, and told him, you know, we had some serious challenges.

We had teacher salaries that were second to the bottom. We had a lot of curricular problems that needed to be addressed, and I wanted to know what he thought. And he said, "Well, you know, I've got an Arkansas company. This is where my executives and their families live, and I think improving the schools would be good for my business.' Now, I have to hasten to say Sam Walton did not like taxes, not one bit, but he figured that there needed to be an investment, not just for Arkansas, but for all of America. So he called the heads of the other big companies in Arkansas, like Tyson Foods, and the oil and gas firms, the banks, and they got together, people started calling them The Good Soup Club, and they pushed hard for comprehensive overhaul of the state education system, improving both standards, accountability, as well as teacher compensation. And they agreed to a small increase in the corporate income tax rate to fund that. Legislation passed, and we began to see improvements." [Hillary Clinton remarks to ECGR Grand Rapids, 6/17/13]

Hillary Clinton Said Sam Walton Asked Her to Serve on the Board of Wal-Mart after She Had Gotten to Know Them Working on Education Reform.

"I served on the Board of Wal-Mart for a couple of years. It was kind of funny how it came about. I had known Sam Walton and had worked with him when my husband was Governor of Arkansas and we were trying to reform education, and he was actually a strong supporter of raising the sales tax and raising a very small percentage of the corporate income tax if it would all go into the schools, a little-told story about Sam Walton. I am sure he is rolling over, sorry that I am telling you. But he and I built up a very close working relationship, and in the late 1980s, probably about '86, he called me one day and he goes, Hillary Clinton, my wife and my daughter think I need a woman on the Board and I can't think of anybody else. I said, Well, you sure know how to flatter me, don't you" [Remarks at London Drug Toronto, 11/4/13]

Wal-Mart 219

Hillary Clinton: "I Had the Most Amazing Experience Serving on the Board and Working with Sam, Because They Were Always Looking over the Horizon."

"But of course I said yes, and I had the most amazing experience serving on the Board and working with Sam, because they were always looking over the horizon. They were always thinking about what came next. Yes, they may have started in small towns and rural areas, in places like Arkansas, but they were always improving their technology. They were among I think the first, if not the first, of, you know, retailers to go into satellite communication and then whatever came next." [Remarks at London Drug Toronto, 11/4/13]

Hillary Clinton Said People Can Criticize Wal-Mart, "but Those Stores Served a Real Purpose, Not Only for Employment and Low Cost Goods, but They Did Become a Way for People Who Wanted to See What Else Was Available to Them Could Go and Look."

"I mention that because those stores—you know, you don't have to agree with everything Wal-Mart does, I don't—but those stores served a real purpose, not only for employment and low cost goods, but they did become a way for people who wanted to see what else was available to them could go and look, products that never were readily available in a lot of those places before. So this spirit of community that I think is absolutely essential to the maintenance of our democracy, our freedom, our strength, is alive and well across North America, particularly among young people." [Remarks at London Drug Toronto, 11/4/13]

Hillary Clinton Said It Was a "Shame" That Wal-Mart Withdrew from India Because of Its Regulatory System.

"I think that if India can ever get its regulatory system straightened out, you know, we have gone back and forth on opening up to retailers, large, multinational retailers. Wal-Mart just withdrew and it is a real shame and because one of the things Wal-Mart promised to do was to help set up the supply chain for agricultural products to actually get to the end user consumer. The harvest in India loses about 40 percent because there is no good storage; there is certainly no good cold storage. So if there is a way to get the politics to open up somewhat in India, you know, the market is just overwhelmingly large." [Remarks at London Drug Toronto, 11/4/13]

INDEX

A

Asia, 61, 120, 143, 159, 160

B

Benghazi, ix, 3, 4, 5, 6
budget, 2, 177

C

campaign contributions, 11
China, 15, 17, 18, 19, 20, 49, 50, 68, 73, 97,
    99, 173
Clinton Foundation, 24, 25
Cuba, 29

D

debt limit, v, 35

E

education, 37, 213, 215, 217, 218

Egypt, 40, 41, 42, 43, 44, 45, 128
Emanuel, Rahm, 55
embassy, 21
energy, 59, 60, 61, 63, 66, 68, 204
Europe, 67, 68

G

Gaddafi, 3
Goldman Sachs, 1, 212
guns, 81

H

Haiti, 83
health care, 86, 87, 91, 95
housing, 204, 206

I

immigration, 145, 148
Iran, 73, 123, 124, 184
Islam, 41
Israel, 128

222 *Index*

J

Japan, 129, 162

L

Libya, 3, 4, 6, 185

M

marijuana, vi, 131
media, vi, 135

N

new economy, vii, 195
North Korea, 18, 137

P

politics, vii, 145, 148, 177, 186
pro-free trade, vii, 155

R

reducing regulations, vii, 165
refugees, 187

Russia, 49, 50, 61, 73, 170, 171

S

Simpson-Bowles, 175, 176
Syria, 179, 180, 182, 185, 186, 188, 189

T

taxes, 90
technology, vii, 24, 51, 58, 59, 66, 110, 195, 216
terrorism, 120, 197

U

unpaid internships, vii, 199

W

Wall Street, 203, 211
Wal-Mart, 213, 214, 217, 218, 219
wealth, 114
WikiLeaks, 74, 75, 77, 79, 80